The Write

Baby and Toddler

Words

D1609616

The Write

Baby and Toddler

Words

poetry, quotes, crafty sayings and scriptures
for all life's little moments

selected by

Crystal Dawn Perry

Crystal Creations
Hixson, Tennessee

The Write

Baby and Toddler

Words

A special thanks to the contributing poets for giving of themselves and their work to this compilation. Every effort has been made to give proper credit for each poem and quote. In the event of any question, we regret the error and will be glad to give proper credit in future editions of this book. The bible scriptures are from the New International Version and the New King James Version.

The Write Baby and Toddler Words
Crystal Creations
P.O. Box 606-B
Hixson, TN. 37343

EK Success Ltd. • P.O. Box 1141 • Clifton, NJ 07014 • www.eksuccess.com

I dedicate this book to my Baby Sunshine.
Your perpetual shining smile brightens my everyday.

Poetry is all that is worth remembering in life.
-William Hazlitt

A few suggestions for getting the most out of

The Write Baby and Toddler Words:

1. Use the cross-references. Cross-references are used when the verses for another topic are suitable but are too numerous to repeat the entire list under both headings. Ex. - When searching the "Sibling" quotes, you will notice a cross-reference to "Multiples." Initially, this may not seem relevant to your subject but if you dismiss this suggestion, you may miss out on the perfect words you were hoping to express.

2. The blank lines found after the "Poetry" and "Quotes, Crafty Sayings, and Scriptures" sections should be used to jot down inspired craft ideas or additional verses.

3. Don't be afraid to change or omit a word, or even an entire line, to suit your needs. These poems and verses are for your personal use – personalize them!

Poetry
T A B L E   O F   C O N T E N T S
for all of life's little moments

Quotes, Crafty Sayings and Scriptures

TABLE OF CONTENTS

for all of life's little moments

The love of a baby is the poetry of life.

-*Crystal Dawn Perry*

Poetry

ADOPTION / FOSTER CHILD

I was just a thought
Not a whisper could I make
God looked down and saw
You had all that you could take.

He knew where I was,
No need to search the lands
He picked me up and kissed me
As he placed me in your hands.

This kiss will be remembered
Each time that you kiss me.
I know this kiss means love
Unconditional, eternally.

If there is not a Heaven
Then how should I believe
That I came to be so blessed
With this family I received?
            -Crystal Dawn Perry

Though you were born
Unto another
I was blessed enough
To become your mother.

Throughout my life
I'll cherish this role
For you have touched
My heart and soul.
            -Aparna Dyer

My heart felt something missing.
At the time, I didn't know that "something"
Would become my reason for living.
I don't know why our life together began so far apart.
How could I have known
A faraway land held the missing beat of my heart?
From distant places with stranger's faces

Our hearts were destined to meet.
Without you for me and me for you
Our lives would not have been complete.
-*Crystal Dawn Perry*

The sweetest gift we've ever known
Came home with us today
To join our little family
A new era underway.

A treasure unimaginable
Entrusted to our care
A precious life to share our love
The answer to our prayer.
-*Brenda Darlene Kijowski*

Fearful, lonely child,
Your crying is through.
Sweet lost soul,
Our search found you.
The world has you asking,
"Where is my place?"
I see the hurt in your eyes,
Trepidation on your face.
As hard times fade into easier,
You will certainly come to know
There is nothing we want more
Than for your hidden smile to grow.
Please believe you are a blessing;
We already know it's true.
We'll love, strengthen, and guide you
To show this truth to you.
-*Crystal Dawn Perry*

One of us, I'm proud to be
He, she, we, them and me,
This awesome family
Blended perfectly.
-*Crystal Dawn Perry*

I've waited so long
To have you to hold
But now I clearly see
God was making arrangements
For you to be with me.
-*Crystal Dawn Perry*

ATTITUDE

Have you heard the platitude
That life is mainly attitude?
With the lift of your chin
And your sneakiest grin
Attitude is what you exude!
-*Aparna Dyer*

Did you see my little foot
Stomping on the ground?
Come on Momma, I'm ready…
Let's go another round.
-*Dana Roberts Clark*

AUNT

I love her more and more
'Cause she never tells me, "You can't."
She is someone special that I adore.
She is my ever-loving AUNT!
-*Crystal Dawn Perry*

BABY
(*see also Birth and Child/Children*)

I never thought I could love someone
The way that I love you.
It's impossible to put into words
But I love you that much; it's true.

I loved you before I saw your face
And before I knew of your charms
But when I looked in your eyes,
You found your place
Deep in my heart and safe in my arms.
-Gina Marie Lauchner

Welcome to the world
It's going to be quite a show.
First, there's something important
I want you to always know:
You are my shining moon; you are my glistening sun.
You are my inner peace; you are my abundant fun.
You are my roaming land; you are my wavy sea,
You are, and always will be, everything to me.
-Crystal Dawn Perry

Bringing you home to
A world that is new
Can you sense how we have
Ached to share it with you?

They say if you wish upon a star,
Your dreams will come true.
In this family, you are the star
And our dreams were for you.
-Crystal Dawn Perry

10 perfect fingers and 10 perfect toes
Mommy's eyes and
Daddy's nose
A wonderful miracle
From Heaven above
Oh, little baby,
How much you are loved!
-Dana Roberts Clark

Eyes of wonder
Skin so fair
Button nose
Silky hair

Bowed lips
Dimpled chin
Delicate fingers
One to ten

Chubby knees
Body round
Kicking feet
Giggling sounds

Soul smiles
Spirit sings
Vibrant charm
Love springs

Joyful nature
Life's heartstring
Sweet perfection
My everything.

-Crystal Dawn Perry

Feed me, change me, wipe my nose,
Give me a nap, and wash my clothes,
Bathe me, walk me, leave me never,
Hug me, love me, I'm yours forever.

-Laura Taylor Mark

He does not say much
Can become quite demanding
And the sound of his cry
Remains most commanding.

Tall, dark and handsome
Can never compete
With the love of my life
Short, bald and sweet.

My pint-sized sweetheart
My baby bugaboo
The light of my life
How much I love you!
-Brenda Darlene Kijowski

Gurgles and boo-boos
Giggles and goo-goos
Grumbles, gas bubbles
Ga-ga's and no-no's
Da-da's and oh-no's
Pat-a-cake, peek-a-boos,
Got your nose!
-Gina Marie Lauchner

I didn't know what to expect
The first time I saw your face
But I fell in love with you instantly
No one will ever take your place.
-Dana Roberts Clark

I was just a thought
Not a whisper could I make
God looked down and saw
You had all that you could take.

He knew where I was,
No need to search the lands.
He picked me up and kissed me
As he placed me in your hands.

This kiss will be remembered
Each time that you kiss me.
I know this kiss means love
Unconditional, eternally.

If there is not a Heaven
Then how should I believe
That I came to be so blessed
With this family I received?
-Crystal Dawn Perry

BABY SHOWER

The cards are stacked
And the presents wrapped.
A nice maternity outfit
Holds my belly trapped.

Receiving blankets and bibs,
Clothes that are tiny and nice
Given with lots of love
And, of course, a little advice.

With friends and family,
We meet to celebrate
The pending arrival
We anxiously await.
    -Crystal Dawn Perry

From friends with love,
From family with love,
Given in love,
For the baby we love.
    -Crystal Dawn Perry

BALLS

Basketballs, baseballs, any kind of ball,
Just throw me one and I'll have fun.
Big balls, little balls any ball at all,
If I'm playing ball, my smiles have just begun.
Light ones, bright ones; I'll catch them all.
I think I may go pro; let me show you how it's done.
    -Crystal Dawn Perry

B A T H

Oh, how I love to take a bath
I splash my feet and it makes me laugh
It's like I've got my own little ocean
I feel so fresh from the soap and the lotion
I'm squeaky clean from my head to my toes
And ready to take on the world...
After I get on some clothes.

-Gina Marie Lauchner

Feed me, change me, wipe my nose,
Give me a nap, and wash my clothes,
Bathe me, walk me, leave me never,
Hug me, love me, I'm yours forever.

-Laura Taylor Mark

Splish splash in the bath
Mommy makes it fun
Squeaky toys, tickley bubbles
Please, don't say we're done!

-Laura Taylor Mark

An empty bathtub, cold and white,
Transforms when you come near.
It rejoices at the sight,
Of a little one so dear.

The coldness goes away,
With one flash of your smile.
Its bubbling water seems to say,
"Will you stay a while?"

You hide behind its curtain,
Playing peek-a-boo,
But you're never really certain,
Whether I'll find you.

The rubber ducky swims along,
Not knowing what else to do,
And then you sing your favorite song,
And ducky starts singing too!

You splash the water to and fro,
And then you start to yawn,
This bath time play is really fun,
But you woke up at dawn!

The warming water is replaced,
By my warm arms instead.
You wrap your legs around my waist,
And I carry you off to bed.

-Aparna Oyer

Wrapped up in a blanket
Cozy, safe and sound
You pick me up and smile
Then you strip me down.
You put me in water
And expect me not to scream
Well, I'll just tell you frankly,
Only in your dreams.
Don't wash behind my ears
And leave my toes alone.
Just because I'm crying,
Try not to use that tone.
Please give me back my blanket.
Wrap me up so tight.
With lots of hugs and kisses,
I'll forgive you...I just might.

-Dana Roberts Clark

BEAUTY / CUTE

You are an undeniable beauty,
The world warmed by your radiance.
Your eyes sparkle and intrigue.
Your smile brightens and enchants.
Watching your beauty, inside and out
I say, "Thank you, Dear Angel,
You have taught my soul to dance."

-Crystal Dawn Perry

Eyelashes sweeping pouty cheeks
Wisps of hair, here and there
A perfect nose above pink, bowed lips
A beautiful face beyond compare.
-Crystal Dawn Perry

Cute as a button I've always heard
But I've always thought they were just words
Because there's no way a button could be
As cute as you are to me.
-Dana Roberts Clark

I love my baby doll.
I like to serve her tea.
My baby doll is really cute
But she's not as cute as me!
-Crystal Dawn Perry

BIG BED

I used to lie in my baby crib
And every night I would grow
So now it's time for a big-kid bed.
The crib has got to go.

Now I can climb up in my bed.
I can get there by myself.
It used to be, someone picked me up,
Like I was being placed upon a shelf.

Is it me or does it seem
That it will be easy to explore
All the things in my room
From the corners to the door?

I think I'll like this arrangement
Yes, I think I might
You can give me a kiss now
It's time to say, "Night Night."
-Crystal Dawn Perry

BIRTH / NEWBORN

Five little fingers on the right and left
Ten tiny toes on two chubby feet
Dimples and rolls and curls so sweet-
All adorably arranged and set in my arms
To trace your cheeks and smell your hair
And whisper, "I love you" with every sigh
Blissfully content to gaze on you,
Watching for that first hint of smile.
-Connie Berry

Daddy doesn't know it
But I'm coming out today.
Mommy has a tingling in
Her tummy where I stay.

I know that he's been waiting
For my Mommy just to say,
"Take me to the hospital...
Our baby's on the way!"

"Call the paramedics,
Call the doctor, Grandma too!
Don't forget the suitcase...
Baby's making his debut!"
-Brenda Darlene Kijowski

I didn't know what to expect
The first time I saw your face
But I fell in love with you instantly.
No one will ever take your place.
-Dana Roberts Clark

Welcome to the world
It's going to be quite a show.
First, there's something important
I want you to always know:
You are my shining moon; you are my glistening sun.
You are my inner peace; you are my abundant fun.
You are my roaming land; you are my wavy sea,
You are, and always will be, everything to me.
-Crystal Dawn Perry

BIRTH DEFECT
(see Hardship)

BIRTHDAY

The older you get the more you hold on
But before you know it the day is gone.
Cherish each smile, each laugh, and each tear.
You blink your eyes and one day becomes a year.
-Dana Roberts Clark

Some birthdays can be exciting
Others are just great fun
But today yours is really special –
It's your first one!
John Beith

I used to hold your bottle
Now you hold it by yourself.
You've just begun to toddle
And pull your toys off the shelf.

We hardly use your stroller
'Cause you're walking on your own.
You've grown your first molar
You're even talking on the phone.

It's only been a year
And look at all that you can do.
I wipe away a tear
As I imagine you at two.
-Aparna Dyer

I would like to have a birthday
Every single day
And a party with cake and ice cream.
Would that be okay?
A candle to blow out
Some gifts to unwrap
We could play games every day
I would just love that!
We could get decorations
Or rent some, or borrow.
We better send invitations
For another party tomorrow!
-Gina Marie Lauchner

It's time for a cake
Some candles
Hooray!
Today is my 3rd birthday!
-Dana Roberts Clark

BIRTHMARK

Here it is for all to see –
God reached down and
Laid his hand on me.
This birthmark he did adorn
To announce to the world
On the day I was born:
God has reached out
And left this mark
To symbolize the way that
I'll reach out
And touch your heart.
-Crystal Dawn Perry

BLANKET

More than a blanket;
More than a covering;
My protector, my comfort,
My friend in discovery.

Always found with me;
Always by my side;
I carry my blankie
Morning, noon, and night.
-Crystal Dawn Perry

The life of a toddler is not as easy as it seems
There are issues such as forgotten diapers, sharing,
And being the target of brother's screams.
Everyday there are stumped toes, wild emotions,
And the occasional skinned knee,
Ladies in the stores commenting on my hair bow
Then asking, "How old is HE?"
Now that I've explained this
I'm sure that you can see
Why a girl must have her blankie
In desperate times such as these.
-Crystal Dawn Perry

[substitute for boy:]
Ladies in the stores commenting on my baseball cap
Then asking, "How old is SHE?"

Upside down, turn around,
Spinning round and round,
Make a face, play pat-a-cake,
Tumble to the ground

Building blocks, wind-up clocks,
Soft toys on a blankie,
Pretty soon it's naptime for
A very tired Mommy!
-Laura Taylor Mark

BLOCKS

(see also Toys)

Stacked up they make a building.
A few more will make a town.
It took skill to get them up.
It takes FUN to knock them down!
-Crystal Dawn Perry

BOOK

You look so cute sitting there
"Reading" your new book.
You start to say the words out loud
But then you make me look.
All the time you've been looking at it
You've had it upside down.
I start to laugh, then you laugh too
But then you make a frown.
What's so funny, Mommy?
You seem to want to say.
Nothing's wrong, honey...
You just made Mommy's day!

-Laura Taylor Mark

Each time we open a book
Your eyes just look and look.
With each page we are turning
More and more you are learning.
I can hardly wait to see
What you do with these things
That are all so new to you.

Joy C. Little

BOTTLE

I used to hold your bottle
Now you hold it by yourself.
You've just begun to toddle
And pull your toys off the shelf.

We hardly use your stroller
'Cause you're walking on your own.
You've grown your first molar;
You're even talking on the phone.

It's only been a year
And look at all that you can do.
I wipe away a tear
As I imagine you at two.

-Aparna Dyer

The life of a toddler is not as easy as it seems
There are issues such as forgotten diapers, sharing,
And being the target of brother's screams.
Everyday there are stumped toes, wild emotions,
And the occasional skinned knee,
Ladies in the stores commenting on my hair bow
Then asking, "How old is HE?"
Now that I've explained this
I'm sure that you can see
Why a girl must have her bottle
In desperate times such as these.

-Crystal Dawn Perry

[substitute for girl:]
Ladies in the stores commenting on my baseball cap
Then asking, "How old is SHE?"

BOYS

(see Son)

BREAST FEEDING

I hold the honor
Of having you close to my chest.

I hold the honor
Of nourishing you best.

I hold the honor
Of feeling your breath.

I hold the honor
Of this life I've been blessed.

-Crystal Dawn Perry

BROTHER

(see also Sibling)

Mom just had a new baby
He doesn't do a lot
Just seems to lie and sleep all day
And is crying when he's not
Mom says when he gets older
He'll want to play with me
But I'm not sure I'll let him
We'll have to wait and see
Still...I suppose it's not so bad
Having a new baby brother
'Cause if I don't really like him
I'll just swap him for another.

–John Beith

I've been blessed to have
A brother like you.
You're my pal, my buddy,
And my best friend too.

–Dana Roberts Clark

Precious brother can you see
What the Lord has given you and me?
The chance to grow and find our way;
But, still we cannot stay away.

Not just a name upon a tree
The Lord has made us family.
To share our lives both good and bad,
To come together happy or sad.

A helping hand within our grasp,
A friendship that you know will last.
Not just a name upon a tree;
The Lord has made us family.

Thankful I shall always be,
The Lord has made you brother to me.

–Brenda Darlene Kijowski

Everyone says
I'm such a great big brother.
That's just the sort of thing
I want to hear from my mother.
I wouldn't trade my job for anything else
Though sometimes,
I want my Mom all to myself.
-Gina Marie Lauchner

CAT
(see also Pet)

My kitty is so special
She's such a loving pet
She knows when I am happy
And she knows when I'm upset.
-Linda Price

My tiny fingers grab your tail
You hiss and spit; I cry and wail!
You see this boo-boo? You caused that!
You silly little cat.
-Carl Joseph Vonnoh, III

CHILD / CHILDREN
(see also Baby and Multiples)

You make me laugh, you make me cry
Oh, little one of mine
You are my light, you are my life
My little ray of sunshine.
-Laura Taylor Mark

The older they get the more you hold on
But before you know it the day is gone.
Cherish each smile, each laugh, and each tear
You blink your eyes and one day becomes a year.
-Dana Roberts Clark

You are my shining moon; you are my glistening sun.
You are my inner peace; you are my abundant fun.
You are my roaming land; you are my wavy sea,
You are, and always will be, everything to me.
-Crystal Dawn Perry

I love you, my sweet child
Please know that this is true
Every little thing about you,
All the special things you do

I love you so much, Mommy
Please know that this is true
All the hugs and kisses,
And the tender I love you's
-Dana Roberts Clark

You are my star,
You shine so bright.
When my heart gets dark,
You send me light.
-Dana Roberts Clark

CHRISTENING / DEDICATION

May God watch over you
And keep you safe
From any dangers
You might face.

May God guide you
And light the way
As you join with Him
On this special day.
-John Beith

The holy water really glistened
On your tender forehead
On the day that you were christened
And the minister said,

"God bless this darling little baby,
Dressed in a gown of white,
And help the parents teach this baby
The Way, The Truth, and The Light."
-Aparna Oyer

CHRISTMAS
(see also Santa Claus)

Pretty boxes, pretty bows,
All stacked in nice neat rows.
I tear open one.
I rip open two.
Uh-oh...
I don't think I was supposed to!
Joy C. Little

Hey! This is my first Christmas.
Just what do you expect?
There are all these pretty boxes
That you want me to wreck.
Can I look at the paper
And pull at the red bow?
No! No! No! Don't tear it up!
Give it back. Let go!
-Dana Roberts Clark

Surrounded by pretty gifts and lights
Ornaments and candles in the night
I find myself fighting back a tear
Overjoyed at our angel this year
Although a Christmas angel is customary
You've given new life to the word, "Merry!"
-Crystal Dawn Perry

COLORING

Look at the pretty picture, Mommy
I made it just for you.
Mommy, don't look at me that way...
The wall looks nice in blue.
-Laura Taylor Mark

Red, yellow, green, blue...
A brand new experience for you.
What will you make?
What will you create?
Oh, well. My mistake...
For the crayons you just ate!
Joy C. Little

COMING HOME

Home from the hospital, your first night here
As I caressed your face and held you near
I noticed that in my palm, I could hold your tiny feet.
This must have been the night that I fell asleep.

When I awoke, I heard you cry for me.
You are a toddler. Where is my baby?
Has this much time really passed
Or are you growing exceedingly fast?

As I think of the first days again
Certainly, the days seem a dream
Yesterday, you were my heart's glisten.
Today, my heart's lively gleam.
 -Crystal Dawn Perry

Bringing you home to
A world that is new
Can you sense how we have
Ached to share it with you?

They say if you wish upon a star,
Your dreams will come true.
In this family, you are the star
And our dreams were for you.
 -Crystal Dawn Perry

My first night at home
Was really just fine.
I woke up Mommy
Only twenty-nine times.
 -Carl Joseph Vonnoh, OOO

Look, I don't require much
Let's get it right this time
I know we just got home
And I like this room of mine
But every time I cry
You must come right away
I'll give you 30 seconds
Before I ruin your day

I'll spit up on your shirt
And then I'll make you late
I'll cry for hours at a time
To see how much you can take
I'll let you get fast asleep
Before I wail again
And if you don't come quickly,
I'll start all over again.

-Dana Roberts Clark

COUSINS

People are a dime a dozen
But there's something priceless about a cousin.
It's the kind of closeness you cannot measure
It's a love that should be treasured forever.
People will always come and go
But with a special cousin
A great friendship grows.

-Gina Marie Lauchner

My favorite cousin
My dearest friend
Playing with toys
Playing pretend
Always found together
Like cute bookends.

-Crystal Dawn Perry

CRAWLING

I was pregnant then I blinked my eyes...
And I held you in my arms.
I brought you home then I blinked my eyes...
Your first smile showed me your charms.
I watched you crawl then I blinked my eyes...
You're growing so fast; forgive my cries.
I was pregnant then I blinked my eyes.

-Dana Roberts Clark

If anyone tells you,
"Don't come crawling to me,"
You can rest assured
That it won't be me.

    -Aparna Dyer

One knee pushes
Then the other
There's no need to sweep,
Don't even bother.
I've been practicing
So now I can crawl.
I'll cover every inch
To get crumbs and all.

    -Crystal Dawn Perry

With two hands of butter,
Soft and sweet,
You pat the floor
And slide your knees.

Your bottom goes up,
And your head goes down,
As you try to explore
All that's around.

And as I watch you,
I soon realize
That my very own heart
Is no longer inside.

With your bottom on top,
And your head below,
My heart didn't have
Any place to go,

Than farther and farther
Outside of me,
Chasing your heels
Passionately.

    -Aparna Dyer

The day that I first smiled
And when I learned to crawl
The time I took my first steps
And didn't even fall

My Mommy keeps a record
Of everything I do
How old I was, the date, the time
The thing that I did new.
-Brenda Darlene Kijowski

CRUISING FURNITURE

Pulling up, holding on
It's time to explore.

Maybe I'll find a treasure –
Oh, boy! I have scored!

A marker, a pen, a nearly full cup
I wonder if this will pour?

Cruising furniture is an adventure
And I'm ready to venture more!
-Crystal Dawn Perry

CRYING / COLIC

He does not say much
Can become quite demanding
And the sound of his cry
Remains most commanding.

Tall, dark and handsome
Can never compete
With the love of my life
Short, bald and sweet.

My pint-sized sweetheart
My baby bugaboo
The light of my life
How much I love you!
-Brenda Darlene Kijowski

I used to listen to the weather,
But lately I don't seem to care.
Sunshine and rain no longer matter,
Except in the expression you wear.

When raindrops dare to dampen
The sweet windows of your soul,
Washing away your tender tears
Is my most important goal.

And when the sunshine reappears
In your charming, disarming smile,
I know I'll save that warming image,
In my eternal memory file.

-Aparna Dyer

I'd like to thank the genius
Who handed me the colic.
I don't recall getting in that line
At the baby chain outlet.
Who gave me colic?
It must be a mistake.
I know it's common
But give me a break.
I've got a coupon
For a rattle that will expire
And one for a bottle and a pacifier
I've got a free pass
For diaper rash
But as for the colic,
I'll have to exchange it!

-Gina Marie Lauchner

Back and forth, pace the floor, rocking in a swing
Fussy babies test our love when they begin to "sing"
When they're done crying and finally go to sleep
Weary parents are thankful
This is one habit that baby doesn't keep!

-Laura Taylor Mark

DANCE

Every time I hear music play
It seems my body will not stay
My head starts bopping
Then my legs go hopping
Then I end with
A staggering sway.
-Crystal Dawn Perry

DAUGHTER

She's a little touch of Heaven
Sent down from above.
She's filled our lives with happiness
And our hearts full of love.
-Dana Roberts Clark

My beautiful daughter
I'm proud that your spirit soars
As you find pleasure in life, in toys,
And in the people you adore.

You have a love for discovery;
I hope your wishes will be explored.
On this journey of life, remember...
You couldn't be loved any more.
-Crystal Dawn Perry

Tiny toes
Ribbon and bows
Bright sparkling eyes
And satin sash ties
Frills and finery fitted with finesse
Perfectly suited for our precious princess.
-Connie Berry

Now I lay me down to sleep
And say a little prayer.
I hope to God that I wake up
With a head of hair.

I don't care if it is straight
And doesn't have any curl.
I just want everyone to know
That I really am a girl!
-Aparna Dyer

I looked ahead in time today
And saw a little girl at play.
So much like her daddy...
So much like her mother...
Yet, so much herself and like no other.
-Teresa E. Glascock

My little girl is growing up
Right before my very eyes
She's a loving mommy to her "baby"
And it comes as no surprise
As she kisses her on the forehead
And gives her a big hug
Exactly the way I do to her,
I feel my heartstrings tug.
I'm glad that she is learning
How to love and be so caring
And I know I'm doing right
With this little life I'm sharing.
-Laura Taylor Mark

I love to clothe my baby girl
In pretty pink dresses
And put little lacy bows
On her silky tresses.

She looks like a little rose
That's beginning to bloom.
She's like a brilliant ray of light
That brightens up the room.
-Aparna Dyer

I wanted to have a daughter
So I could pass down a few things
Like keepsakes, favorite china
And maybe my special rings
Heritage traditions, family photos
And a well-loved favorite toy
Will be stored away for you to someday
Show your own pride and joy
Most importantly I hope the
Unconditional love in all I do
Will be the most treasured gift
That you take away with you.
  -Laura Taylor Mark

The most precious gift
From Heaven above
Is the gift of a daughter
For a mother to love.
  -Dana Roberts Clark

A daughter is a dream come true.
Pink lace, ribbons, fluff and froufrou,
Giggles, kisses, bubbles and bows,
She's such a sweet dear from her head to her toes!
  -Laura Taylor Mark

DAY CARE / PRE - SCHOOL

Finances seem to limit
My choice at home to stay
So I trust my precious package
To daycare through the day.
  -Brenda Darlene Kijowski

Although I know this is a good step
For your budding life's preparation.
It is not easy for either of us...
We both abide the separation.

You will play, paint, color, learn,
Explore on a pretend adventure.
It is time to turn from my trusty hand
Into the trusted hands of your teacher.

I know you will learn; you are very smart.
Friends will abound from your luring charm.
It is not these things I worry about,
But for now, you are not in my arms.
    -Crystal Dawn Perry

I know you will paint and play
And meet some new friends
But the pain in my heart
Feels like it will not end.

You won't see tears fall down my face
But if you could look inside,
You would see a river flowing
Because I must say "Good-bye."
    -Dana Roberts Clark

Learning to play
Learning to share
Making first friends
And learning to care
Playdates with children
You have come to adore
Each day spent together
Leaves them loving you more.
    -Crystal Dawn Perry

DIAPERS

The diaper is in hand
But what she doesn't understand
Is I'm the fastest in the west
I can make it fly the best
The diaper is off and here I go
It made it to her face...what a show!
    -Dana Roberts Clark

I know it's just a phase
You will grow out of in time
But it seems every time I see you
Your birthday suit shines
I dress you everyday
I put on your socks and shoes
I turn around and you're naked
Even your diaper is off too!
-Dana Roberts Clark

It's certainly a dirty job
But as a parent, it's my duty.
Changing your diaper does have benefits –
I get to see the world's cutest booty!
-Crystal Dawn Perry

DIMPLES

Like big, beautiful diamonds flashed,
They are a sight to see.
I am undeniably impressed,
Though there's a hint of jealousy.
These sparklers are not actually worn
On your finger, the usual place.
The dazzle seems to come along
With a smile on your face.
I realize I cannot buy these gems
And the reason is very simple
They are not diamonds at all...
I believe they are called dimples!
-Crystal Dawn Perry

DIRTY / MESSY

Dirty, sticky, downright icky,
Your baby hands are such an awful mess
I've cleaned them umpteen times today
But I don't love you any less!
-Laura Taylor Mark

DOCTOR

Taking your temperature, giving a shot
Asking questions, checking for spots
Listen to your heart, inspecting your ears
Time for your check-up means
Time for your tears.

The tears come naturally with
Your screams and hollers.
This is all typical when
I take you to the doctor.
-Crystal Dawn Perry

DOG
(see also Pet)

A puppy is like another baby
Except it's really furry.
It needs a lot of caring.
It causes lots of worry.
A puppy might be cute and warm
Except when it scratches and chews.
A puppy is like another baby
Except a baby doesn't eat shoes!
-Gina Marie Lauchner

Playful and cuddly,
Paws wet and muddy,
Walks in the sunshine,
Barking in the nighttime,
Fur that needs brushing,
Tricks that need working,
Begging and panting,
Scratching and playing
Comforting and petting,
One of the family.
-Gina Marie Lauchner

D O L L

My little girl is growing up
Right before my very eyes
She's a loving mommy to her "baby"
And it comes as no surprise
As she kisses her on the forehead
And gives her a big hug
Exactly the way I do to her,
I feel my heartstrings tug.
I'm glad that she is learning
How to love and be so caring
And I know I'm doing right
With this little life I'm sharing.
    -Laura Taylor Mark

I love my baby doll.
I like to serve her tea.
My baby doll is really cute
But she's not as cute as me!
    -Crystal Dawn Perry

D R E S S - U P

A little lipstick for my cheeks
I've only just begun!
Eye shadow on my nose and lips
I think that's how it's done...
Being beautiful is sure hard work
But it's also lots of fun!
    -Gina Marie Lauchner

Pearls and boas, dressed to the nines,
Lipstick on pursed lips, trying to stay in the lines.
Big wobbly high heels on tiny, precious feet,
Little girls playing dress up – aren't they sweet!
    -Laura Taylor Mark

Tiny toes
Ribbon and bows
Bright sparkling eyes
And satin sash ties
Frills and finery fitted with finesse
Perfectly suited for our precious princess.
-*Connie Berry*

E A R S

(*see Face*)

E A S T E R

I knew when you woke up on Easter at sunrise
You'd wonder if the Easter Bunny stopped by
We'd wonder how he hopped on past
And filled your basket up so fast
And how did he even have the time
To hide colorful eggs for you to find?
I knew when you woke up you would be surprised
That the Easter Bunny is such a cool guy!
-*Gina Marie Lauchner*

Enjoy the baskets, bunnies, and chickens
But remember to celebrate that
Our Lord Christ has risen!
-*Crystal Dawn Perry*

E A T I N G

Didn't you notice
A bottle makes me hush?
So why did you fill
My mouth with this mush?

For this, you'll see,
Revenge will be mine
The floor will be covered
Along with the high chair and blinds.

You know this is true
But I won't stop there
If you feed another bite
You'll wear it in your hair.

I don't want cereal
And don't even try peas.
Come on, get the hint...
A bottle is fine with me!
-Crystal Dawn Perry

I can't help it if I'm a messy eater
I haven't learned all the tricks
Like how to get the food in my mouth
Or the exact location of my lips.
-Gina Marie Lauchner

It's nasty and it's mushy.
Why are you so pushy?
The more you put in
The more I wear on my chin.
Can't you tell? Don't you know?
Inside, I'm screaming, "No! No! No!"
-Crystal Dawn Perry

Don't you love the bib I'm wearing?
I bet you want one too.
You can borrow it after it's washed
Then it will look "good as new."
I can't help that I'm so stylin';
I'm a fashionable little kid.
And if you think I look cool now
Just wait 'til you check out my crib!
-Gina Marie Lauchner

Feed me, change me, wipe my nose,
Give me a nap, and wash my clothes,
Bathe me, walk me, leave me never,
Hug me, love me, I'm yours forever.
-Laura Taylor Mark

EVERYDAY

A smile here and a frown there,
Sweet moments to share with teddy bears,
Eyes getting big as excitement builds,
Cleaning up all sorts of spills,
A hug and kiss to take your problems away...
What a joy, making memories everyday.
-Dana Roberts Clark

EYES

(see Face)

FACE

Your cherub-like cheeks
So perfectly round
Your tiny bowed lips
Ready to imitate sounds
Watching your zigzag, wobbly run
I know your learning has just begun.
-Crystal Dawn Perry

I gaze into your eyes
And wonder what you see
With those cute little peepers
Intently watching me.

I know you can't see
How very much I love you.
For you, my precious child,
There's nothing I wouldn't do.

Right now, I'm more than happy
To be on the giving end.
I'm sowing seeds of love
In this garden I must tend.

As you grow and change
And find your own way,
I know the love I've given
Will come back to me someday.
          -Laura Taylor Mark

You are an undeniable beauty,
The world warmed by your radiance.
Your eyes sparkle and intrigue.
Your smile brightens and enchants.
Watching your beauty, inside and out
I say, "Thank you, Dear Angel,
You have taught my soul to dance."
          -Crystal Dawn Perry

Eyelashes sweeping pouty cheeks
Wisps of hair, here and there
A perfect nose above pink, bowed lips
A beautiful face beyond compare.
          -Crystal Dawn Perry

10 perfect fingers and 10 perfect toes
Mommy's eyes and
Daddy's nose
A wonderful miracle
From Heaven above
Oh, little baby,
How much you are loved!
          -Dana Roberts Clark

Eyes of wonder
Skin so fair
Button nose
Silky hair

Bowed lips
Dimpled chin
Delicate fingers
One to ten

Chubby knees
Body round
Kicking feet
Giggling sounds

Soul smiles
Spirit sings
Vibrant charm
Love springs

Joyful nature
Life's heartstring
Sweet perfection
My everything.
-Crystal Dawn Perry

Have you HEARD the news?
Lend me your EARS...
The best time of your life
Is your EAR-ly years.
-Crystal Dawn Perry

Gurgles and boo-boos
Giggles and goo-goos
Grumbles, gas bubbles
Ga-ga's and no-no's
Da-da's and oh-no's
Pat-a-cake, peek-a-boos,
Got your nose!
-Gina Marie Lauchner

Feed me, change me, wipe my nose,
Give me a nap, and wash my clothes,
Bathe me, walk me, leave me never,
Hug me, love me, I'm yours forever.
-Laura Taylor Mark

FAMILY / FAMILY
TREE / HERITAGE

The love and care
Does so overflow;
The love in our family
Is the heart of our home.
  -Crystal Dawn Perry

For the good times
And bad
Memories we've had,
I
Love
You!
  -Crystal Dawn Perry

Someday you will know
Just how you came to be
What branch you fall upon
In our family tree
You'll look at all the pictures
And point your little fingers
At family members who used to live
And now to you, are strangers
Their legacy will live on in you
And someday you will see
A little face looking up at you,
Another branch in the tree.
  -Laura Taylor Mark

I wanted to have a daughter
So I could pass down a few things
Like keepsakes, favorite china
And maybe my special rings
Heritage traditions, family photos
And a well-loved favorite toy
Will be stored away for you to someday
Show your own pride and joy
Most importantly I hope the
Unconditional love in all I do
Will be the most treasured gift
That you take away with you.
  -Laura Taylor Mark

FATHER
(see also Parenthood)

When it's Daddy's time to play with you
It's your favorite time of all
You get to show him how you sit up
And how you're learning to crawl

You get to play peek-a-boo
And laugh whenever you fall
You get to show him how you spit up –
You and Daddy have a ball!
        -Gina Marie Lauchner

One of the most precious gifts
From Heaven above
Is the gift of a daughter
For a Daddy to love.
        -Dana Roberts Clark

Don't worry Daddy
I'll teach you what to do.
I'll show you the ropes from
Diapers to boo-boos.

You've got a good head start.
You've mastered my first rule.
The first rule is this...
My daddy must be cool!
        -Crystal Dawn Perry

We understand each other
My daddy and me
Although I'm only one month old
We have a special bond, you see
People say I'm just like him
And I really must agree
'Cause Daddy is always sleeping
And has gas...just like me!
        -John Beith

I looked ahead in time today
And saw a little girl at play.
So much like her daddy...
So much like her mother...
Yet, so much herself and like no other.
-Teresa E. Glascock

When Daddy throws me in the air,
It gives me such an awful scare.
When I come down, he catches me.
I want to cry, but I say, "Wheee!"
-Laura Taylor Mark

Devoted
Always
Dedicated
Dignified
Youthful
-Crystal Dawn Perry

FEET

Ten tiny toes on
Two softly padded feet
Symbols of innocence ...
What will they carry you to meet?
-Crystal Dawn Perry

Five little fingers on the right and left
Ten tiny toes on two chubby feet
Dimples and rolls and curls so sweet-
All adorably arranged and set in my arms
To trace your cheeks and smell your hair
And whisper, "I love you" with every sigh
Blissfully content to gaze on you,
Watching for that first hint of smile.
-Connie Berry

Eyelashes resting on pouty cheeks
Ten precious toes on two precious feet
From head to toe, from toe to head
The world's most precious angel
Lies sleeping in your bed.
    -Crystal Dawn Perry

10 perfect fingers and
10 perfect toes
Mommy's eyes and
Daddy's nose
A wonderful miracle
From Heaven above
Oh, little baby,
How much you are loved!
    -Dana Roberts Clark

GIRLS
(see Daughter)

GODCHILD / GODPARENTS

The world was searched
For the perfect person
But instead, an angel was sent...
Providing security to our lives
Offering promised love
By being a loving Godparent.
    -Crystal Dawn Perry

I will hold you in my arms
And coddle you with utmost charm.
Safe shall you be from all alarm,
My precious little Godchild.
    -Carl Joseph Vonnoh, III

GRANDCHILDREN/ GRANDPARENTS

Send up the fireworks!
Strike up the band!
Tell the whole world...
You are the essence of GRAND!
-Crystal Dawn Perry

My Grandpa and I are alike in many ways
He laughs like I do whenever he plays
He smiles like me, and we both smile a lot
He has sparkle in his eyes –
That's something else I've got!
-Gina Marie Lauchner

A copy of a copy
Will surely disappoint.
Videos and documents
Are cases in point.

The only time an original
Should be copied twice,
Is when a person
Is especially nice.

That person needs to make
A baby-faced clone,
And that clone should make another
Clone of her own.

The result will truly be
A spectacular sight,
For this copy of a copy
Will be a grand delight!
-Aparna Dyer

I was pregnant then I blinked my eyes...
And I held you in my arms.
I brought you home then I blinked my eyes...
Your first smile showed me your charms.
I watched you crawl then I blinked my eyes...
And you were running down the hall.
Your first day at school then I blinked my eyes...
I heard your first boyfriend call.
Sweet sixteen came then I blinked my eyes...
Your dad bought you an old car.
Your college life began then I blinked my eyes...
You've always been our shining star.
Dad walked you down the aisle then I blinked my eyes.
You've grown up so fast forgive my cries.
You are pregnant then I blinked my eyes...
-Dana Roberts Clark

I am lucky I have a Grandma
Who loves me so so much
My Grandma is so special
She has a special touch
She loves me more than anything
And I love her a bunch
I love it when we share a snack
And when she makes me lunch.
-Gina Marie Lauchner

Finances seem to limit
My choice at home to stay
So I trust my precious package
To Grandparents through the day.
-Brenda Darlene Kijowski

Grandma's gonna spoil me
And let me have my way
With all the things Mommy
Says "No" to every day!
-Laura Taylor Mark

They searched the heavens, near and far;
Inside each cloud, on every star.
To heavens all, a sad dismay;
A special angel had gone astray.
The Lord did finally look on down,
And see a twinkle on this ground.
A message rose from earth that day,
As Grandpa smiled up to say;
"I'm here, My Lord, do not dismay,
This angel has not gone astray."
  -Brenda Darlene Kijowski

GROWING

I was pregnant then I blinked my eyes...
And I held you in my arms.
I brought you home then I blinked my eyes...
Your first smile showed me your charms.
I watched you crawl then I blinked my eyes...
And you were running down the hall.
Your first day at school then I blinked my eyes...
I heard your first boyfriend call.
Sweet sixteen came then I blinked my eyes...
Your dad bought you an old car.
Your college life began then I blinked my eyes...
You've always been our shining star.
Dad walked you down the aisle then I blinked my eyes...
You've grown up so fast forgive my cries.
You are pregnant then I blinked my eyes...
  -Dana Roberts Clark

If I could create
Anything in the world,
What would it be?
I would create a room,
A room of magical memories.
The room would be decorated
Not with pillows, throws, and candles
But with your scent, your giggles,
In the corner, a pair of your baby sandals.
I could go to this room
And feel your tiny arms

Wrapped around my neck;
Once again, mesmerized by your charm.
This place does exist but
It is not a room;
It is my heart, filled with your soul.
It is an escape from the gloom.
As I proudly watch you grow
Smarter, stronger, taller every day
I know that no matter where you go,
No matter how far away,
This place of magical memories
Is where, together, we can stay.
-Crystal Dawn Perry

I dread the day when you are grown
When you can venture out alone.

You won't need me at your side
To hold your hand and be your guide.

You won't need me to chase your fears
To give you a hug and wipe your tears.

I know if I could have just one wish come true
I'd stay "Mommy" forever and you'd stay little you.
-Laura Taylor Mark

Home from the hospital, your first night here
As I caressed your face and held you near
I noticed that in my palm, I could hold your tiny feet.
This must have been the night that I fell asleep.

When I awoke, I heard you cry for me.
You are a toddler. Where is my baby?
Has this much time really passed
Or are you growing exceedingly fast?

As I think of the first days again
Certainly, the days seem a dream
Yesterday, you were my heart's glisten.
Today, my heart's lively gleam.
-Crystal Dawn Perry

HAIR / LACK OF / HAIRCUT

Eyelashes sweeping pouty cheeks
Wisps of hair, here and there
A perfect nose above pink, bowed lips
A beautiful face beyond compare.
-Crystal Dawn Perry

This is the day that
Mommy has dreaded;
I'll still be precious but
I won't be curly-headed!
-Crystal Dawn Perry

The fear...the anxiety...the dread!
There's a sharp pair of scissors
Aimed straight at my head!
I've got to get out of here;
There's nowhere to run.
I guess I'll just Cry! Wiggle! Scream! –
From the top of my lungs!
-Crystal Dawn Perry

Now I lay me down to sleep
And say a little prayer.
I hope to god that I wake up
With a head of hair.

I don't care if it is straight
And doesn't have any curl.
I just want everyone to know
That I really am a girl!
-Aparna Dyer

He does not say much
Can become quite demanding
And the sound of his cry
Remains most commanding.

Tall, dark and handsome
Can never compete
With the love of my life
Short, bald and sweet.

My pint-sized sweetheart
My baby bugaboo
The light of my life
How much I love you!
-Brenda Darlene Kijowski

It is very attractive
But look at all that hair!
Sometimes I wonder...
Is my kid under there?
-Crystal Dawn Perry

HALF - SIBLING

They call us half-brothers
But what I've come to know
Is that it takes these two halves
To make our family whole.
-Crystal Dawn Perry

Different yet alike in so many ways,
It must be true,
That a gesture here or expression there
Can only mean you two
Are just like any "full" siblings would be,
Except what sets you apart
Is the special bond you'll always share,
A loving parent's heart.
-Laura Taylor Mark

One of us, I'm proud to be
He, she, we, them and me,
This awesome family
Blended perfectly.
-*Crystal Dawn Perry*

HALLOWEEN

Some kids are dressed
To scare and spook
But not me...
I'm dressed to be CUTE!
-*Crystal Dawn Perry*

What better night than Halloween
To take my pumpkin out?
I'll make sure that you are seen
Throughout the local route.

You will have a costume handy
And try to appear frightful.
You will get oodles of candy
And it will be delightful!
-*Aparna Dyer*

HANDS

Dirty, sticky, downright icky,
Your baby hands are such an awful mess
I've cleaned them umpteen times today
But I don't love you any less!
-*Laura Taylor Mark*

Five little fingers on the right and left
Ten tiny toes on two chubby feet
Dimples and rolls and curls so sweet –
All adorably arranged and set in my arms
To trace your cheeks and smell your hair
And whisper, "I love you" with every sigh
Blissfully content to gaze on you,
Watching for that first hint of smile.
-*Connie Berry*

10 perfect fingers and 10 perfect toes
Mommy's eyes and
Daddy's nose
A wonderful miracle
From Heaven above
Oh, little baby,
How much you are loved!
-Dana Roberts Clark

Mom and I,
Hand in hand
Could this life
Be any more grand?
-Carl Joseph Vonnoh, OOO

My sister is the coolest!
She plays with me,
She holds my hand,
She walks with me,
She helps me stand.
My sister is the best!
-Carl Joseph Vonnoh, OOO

HANUKKAH

The hand that rocks the cradle
Carefully lights the menorah.
The baby that rocks the dreidel
Listens to me read the Torah.

The ones whom I hold dear
Are passing on tradition
As we gather here
With our new addition.
-Aparna Dyer

HARDSHIP

More disheartening than
Love gone wrong...
An angel without a song.
My drenched heart is broken,
Days unplayed, words unspoken;

The soul of my prayers is
That you will have the chance
To be the star in
Life's most precious dance.
     -Crystal Dawn Perry

How we managed to make it through,
I guess we'll never know,
But I'm grateful that we did it together
Because tough times can help us grow.
We'll find our way; we always will.
As long as we have each other,
You will always be my baby
And I will always be your mother.
     -Gina Marie Lauchner

Watching you, caring for you,
Sending up prayer after prayer.
I cannot hold you often but
My heart is always there.
     -Crystal Dawn Perry

Thanks for taking
The extra time
To care for these
Special needs of mine.
     -Dana Roberts Clark

Hi! My name is Kelsey and I'm going to tell you a story about people that are not like us. Well, you people might think it doesn't matter, but it does to those handecap people. Well, it all starts when someone is born wrong, and when they come to school their afraid what your going to say. They want to be like you, so you have to help them and like them. It doesn't matter if they drool on you, it just means that they are either tired or getting use to you. You people that have brothers and sisters that are handecap, don't be embarrassed when you go in public. If somebody comes up to you and says what's wrong with that person, just say, oh, that's my speical brother or sister. And if they walk away, don't be sad, you still have that speical person. That speical person can't help it, she or he are speical and can have tons of friends. It doesn't matter if there in a handecap class. It just means there speical.

-Kelsey A. Wolfgramm
4th grade

We are doing what we can for you
I don't know why you came so early.
I often said I couldn't wait for you
Maybe you couldn't wait for me.
-Crystal Dawn Perry

You are my star,
You shine so bright.
When my heart gets dark,
You send me light.
-Dana Roberts Clark

HOLDING BABY

Sitting on my lap, with my arms wrapped around you,
I know that I will not always have you to hold
But I hope that no matter how big you get or how far you go
You will always feel my love as you feel my warmth today,
Sitting on my lap, with my arms wrapped around you.
-Crystal Dawn Perry

Five little fingers on the right and left
Ten tiny toes on two chubby feet
Dimples and rolls and curls so sweet –
All adorably arranged and set in my arms
To trace your cheeks and smell your hair
And whisper, "I love you" with every sigh
Blissfully content to gaze on you,
Watching for that first hint of smile.
-Connie Berry

When I've had a day that's taxing,
I hold my baby in my lap.
Nothing could ever be as relaxing
As both of us taking a nap.
-Aparna Dyer

I never thought I could love someone
The way that I love you
It's impossible to put into words
But I love you that much, it's true
I loved you before I saw your face
And before I knew of your charms
But when I looked in your eyes,
You found your place
Deep in my heart and safe in my arms.
-Gina Marie Lauchner

HOME BIRTH

Consoling to my heart
There are no comforts on earth
Like giving you the comfort of home
-an amazing home birth.
-Crystal Dawn Perry

HUGS AND KISSES

Feed me, change me, wipe my nose,
Give me a nap, and wash my clothes,
Bathe me, walk me, leave me never,
Hug me, love me, I'm yours forever.
-Laura Taylor Mark

Happiness when you give one
Understanding when you need one
Great when you receive one
-Dana Roberts Clark

INDEPENDENCE DAY

Send up the fireworks!
Strike up the band!
Tell the whole world...
I'm good... I'm great...
I'm GRAND!
-Crystal Dawn Perry

Today is the day.
Now is the time.
I'll scream really loud.
I'll even whine.
My mommy will see
How it is going to be...
Today I will be free.
-Dana Roberts Clark

Treasured memories
Repeated
Again & again
Deep-rooted
In
Tradition, on our
Independence Day
Of this
Nation
-Crystal Dawn Perry

I N J U R Y

Your wounded knee, all bruised and bleeding
Tears down your cherub cheeks, are streaming
But in my eyes they, too, are gleaming
I feel your pain, my child.

And so I take you in my arms
There is no pain, there's no alarm
I comfort you; I'm safe, I'm warm
I feel your pain, my child.

Now bandaged up, you skip away
I've conquered all that ails today
But remember, as you run and play
I feel your pain, my child.
-Carl Joseph Vonnoh, DDD

Ow! It hurts so much
And it gave me such a scare!
Mommy prescribed a band-aid
And some tender loving care.

Now I'm ready to have fun
From sun-up until the moon.
As long as Mommy is around
Love will heal all wounds.
-Crystal Dawn Perry

Wah! Wah! Boo-hoo!
Baby's got a boo-boo!

What is the diagnosis?
Needs a little hug and kiss

Baby is on the mend.
Now off to play again.
-Crystal Dawn Perry

LAUGHTER

No matter how loud,
No matter how silly
Giggle Ha Ha
Snicker Hee Hee
There's no laugh as cute
As yours is to me.
-*Crystal Dawn Perry*

I carry the tune in my heart.
Daily life it does console.
The sound of your laughter
Is soothing music to my soul.
-*Crystal Dawn Perry*

LOVE

I never thought I could love someone
The way that I love you
It's impossible to put into words
But I love you that much, it's true
I loved you before I saw your face
And before I knew of your charms
But when I looked in your eyes,
You found your place
Deep in my heart and safe in my arms.
-*Gina Marie Lauchner*

I never knew three little words
Could ever mean so much
Until I looked into your eyes
And felt your sweet soft touch.
"I love you."
-*Dana Roberts Clark*

Feed me, change me, wipe my nose,
Give me a nap, and wash my clothes,
Bathe me, walk me, leave me never,
Hug me, love me, I'm yours forever.
-Laura Taylor Mark

The loving times we share,
The special things we do
Are a warm and gentle reminder
Of how much I love you.
-John Beith

MEMORY OF A LOVED ONE

If I could create
Anything in the world,
What would it be?
I would create a room,
A room of magical memories.
The room would be decorated
Not with pillows, throws, and candles
But with your scent, your giggles,
In the corner, a pair of your baby sandals.
I could go to this room
And feel your tiny arms
Wrapped around my neck;
Once again, mesmerized by your charm.
This place does exist but
It is not a room;
It is my heart, filled with your soul.
It is an escape from the gloom.
No matter where I go,
No matter how far away,
This place of magical memories
Is where, together, we can stay.
-Crystal Dawn Perry

Mommy, Mommy, please don't cry.
I know you don't understand why
You'll never hold me in your arms
You'll never see all of my charms.
Never is a word you should never say
Because you can come see me one day.
My Heavenly Father looked at my life

He saw all the pain and all the strife.
So He kept me here with Him to live
And salvation for you He freely gives.
So you can come and live here too.
Mommy, please don't cry, I love you.

-*Dana Roberts Clark*

I cannot see her
But I know she is there.
She's my guardian angel;
My life with me she shares.
Until my time is over
And God wants to bring me home,
She will be there to protect me
When things sometimes go wrong.

-*Dana Roberts Clark*

MOTHER

(see also Parenthood)

I could never imagine
...being a mother.

I could never imagine
...having to take care of someone
so little who needed so much.

I could never imagine
...that I would get you out of
all the mommies in the world.

I could never imagine
...my life without you.

-*Laura Taylor Mark*

I love you my sweet child
Please know that this is true
Every little thing about you,
All the special things you do

I love you so much, Mommy
Please know that this is true
All the hugs and kisses,
And the tender I love you's
-Dana Roberts Clark

From here to the glistening stars
Grass blades numbered in the yard
Baby's beauty beyond compare
Unnoticed whispers in the air
A greater measure, there is no other
As the infinite love of one's own mother.
-Crystal Dawn Perry

Once upon a memory,
Someone wiped away a tear,
Held me close and loved me,
Thank you Mother dear.
-Unknown

Being a mother means...
Being blessed, being tired, prayers sent above
Dreams for your child, hopes thought of,
Emotions recognized, unconditional love,
Never-ending laundry and never-ending love.
-Crystal Dawn Perry

As a mother I am hopeful
That I nurture your hopes and dreams
As a mother I am wishful
That your every wish comes true
As a mother I feel helpless
To help you as I want
As a mother I am honored
To give my best to you.
-Crystal Dawn Perry

I looked ahead in time today
And saw a little girl at play.
So much like her daddy...
So much like her mother...
Yet, so much herself and like no other.
-Teresa E. Glascock

Mom and I,
Hand in hand
Could this life
Be any more grand?
-Carl Joseph Vonnoh, III

MOUTH
(see Face)

MULTIPLES

"How do you do it?" people say
When they see my brood and I.
"They must be lots of work," they say
And shake their heads and sigh.
I smile and say that yes, they are
And worth every single minute.
My world revolves around them
And I can't imagine them not in it!
-Laura Taylor Mark

Two car seats, two dressers
Two strollers, two cribs
A drawer full of diapers
And a drawer full of bibs

Two feedings, two changings
Two lullabies to sing
Two sweet babies cooing
Content in their swings

Double the caring
And the nights without sleep
But, double the joy and
Rewards you shall reap

Two babies to cuddle
Two sweet turtledoves
Two lives now unfolding
Created in love.
   -Brenda Darlene Kijowski

Double the pleasure
Double the fun
Double the chaos
With 2, not just 1.

Double the groceries
Double the food
Double the clothes
They both outgrew.

Double the treasure
It's only just begun
The joy they bring together
Will never be outdone.
   -Gina Marie Lauchner

Two little twins as cute as can be
Each with different personalities.
One will laugh then one will cry.
One will smirk and the other sigh.
One will wave her hands, the other kick her feet.
One will sing a song, and the other makes a beat.
Sleepy as a bear or busy as a bee,
You will always be precious angels to me.
   -Amber D. Clark

NAME

Jessica, Kevin, Kylie or Devon
Cassandra, Zack, Maria or Max
Samantha or Brandon, Amanda or Adam
Shannon or Jarod, Kaitlyn or Aaron
Christina or Jacob, Juanita or Clay
Grace, Alexander, Hannah or Chase
Tracy or Travis, Allisa or Wesley
Kelsey or Justin, Elizabeth or Dustin
Matthew or Mary, Tanner or Amy
Lucas or Kara, Tyler or Emily
Connor, Kelly, William or Danielle
Breanna or Bradley
Jack or Jill?
                    -Gina Marie Lauchner

With a name, I must identify
The person whom you are
A child, young person or adult
A musician, athlete, superstar.

How can I decide so early
What symbol encompasses you?
A name that will be perfect
No matter what you do.

I pray that you approve my choice
This decision, I make for you
For my child, you have not a clue
The struggle I've gone through.
                    -Brenda Darlene Kijowski

Send up the fireworks!
Strike up the band!
I hope the New Year
Will be as grand as I am!
    -Crystal Dawn Perry

NOSE
(see Face)

NUDITY

I know it's just a phase
You will grow out of in time
But it seems every time I see you
Your birthday suit shines
I dress you everyday
I put on your socks and shoes
I turn around and you're naked
Even your diaper is off too!
    -Dana Roberts Clark

Four plump cheeks I see.
Please, come here. I beg.
We better get two covered
Before something runs down your leg!
    -Crystal Dawn Perry

NURSERY

Soft, fuzzy hair on a damp forehead,
Quiet breathing in a soft-lit room,
Baby powder scented air,
Tip-toeing away...longing to stay.
    -Laura Taylor Mark

The doctor can't tell
If you're a girl or a fellow
I guess we'll play it safe
And paint the nursery yellow.
        -Crystal Dawn Perry

I dreamed it, searched, and decorated
With just what I thought you would like,
Cute objects for you to look at
And a bed for comfort at night

I'm proud of it and hope you like it
Here is a nursery of your own
To play in, to dress in, to sleep in
Until bigger you have grown.

You are growing every day
So I know that won't take long
Let's make the most of your nursery,
Decorating memories with lullaby songs.
        -Crystal Dawn Perry

PACIFIER / THUMB

You're always there for me.
You always comfort my cries.
You always help me relax
When I lie in bed at night.
You're always there when
The stress of life is dire.
You are my love...
My dearest friend...
You are my pacifier.
        -Crystal Dawn Perry

Binkies of every size, color and shape
In every bag, purse and pack
Between the cushions of the couch
Under the front seat of the car
In coat pockets, jean pockets and suit pockets
In my desk, in the tub and under my pillow
Yet there's never a binkie in my hand
At the moment we need one most.
    -Connie Berry

What a screamer!
What a crier!
Somebody grab a pacifier!
    -Crystal Dawn Perry

The life of a toddler is not as easy as it seems
There are issues such as forgotten diapers, sharing,
And being the target of brother's screams.
Everyday there are stumped toes, wild emotions,
And the occasional skinned knee,
Ladies in the stores commenting on my hair bow
Then asking, "How old is HE?"
Now that I've explained this
I'm sure you can see
Why a girl must suck her thumb
In desperate times such as these.
    -Crystal Dawn Perry

[substitute for boy:]
Ladies in the stores commenting on my baseball cap
Then asking, "How old is SHE?"

PARENTHOOD

(see also Father and Mother)

Nobody ever sits you down
To explain the rules
There are no schools
Offering parenting tools

No mandatory tests
You have to pass
No exams or
A class on diaper rash

No contract to sign
No personal guide
To stand by your side
When the baby cries

It was easy to discover
The most important rule
That I already knew-
I've got lots of love for you!
-Gina Marie Lauchner

It takes understanding to see
The true worth of the work
And focus on the goal
Not the rut in the road.
It takes courage to be
The parent they need
And patience to see
The days and nights through.
It takes faith in the fact
That this too will pass
And love in the heart
That will forever last.
-Connie Berry

PARK

Today is a big day for you and me
We're going to the park
To see what we can see
A little bird, a tree
And a baby swing for you –
As long as we're together,
It doesn't matter what we do!
-Laura Taylor Mark

PASSOVER

The first-born
Passed over by the Lord
To freedom's way
Passover...
Oh, exalted day!
-Crystal Dawn Perry

PET

Your love is unconditional
Considerate and kind
And best of all, my precious pet,
I'm yours and you are mine.
-Brenda Darlene Kijowski

PLAY / PLAY GROUP
(see Toys)

PLAYPEN

I'm a little jailbird
Longing to be free.
Ain't I the cutest captive
You ever did see?

Yep, I'm in the pen again
What did I do this time?
It seems to me the punishment
Never fits the crime.
-Crystal Dawn Perry

POSING FOR CAMERA

I don't want my picture taken
Not today or any day.
Mommy got me all cleaned up
But I want to run and play!
All right, I'll smile and make a face
That Mommy wants to see.
There now, please! Just let me be!
-Laura Taylor Mark

I'm very cute.
I know I am.
Why do you think
I'm such a ham?

I know a camera
Likes to see beauty.
That's why I pose
And look so pretty.

So go ahead and
Snap a picture.
It's going to be cute.
I know that for sure!
-Crystal Dawn Perry

PREGNANCY

I've read all the books.
I've tried to prepare.
I've done the right things
To give the best care.
Between my passion for you
And enough baby books to share,
There's one subject I'm certain
That no other can compare.
As a Mommy, I'll be a cut above
Not because of my knowledge, but
My all-encompassing love!
-Crystal Dawn Perry

Mommy's belly is getting bigger every day.
I once blew up a balloon the very same way.
Little by little, in went the air
Then my balloon popped everywhere!
I wonder, I do...
Will Mommy's belly pop too?
Joy C. Little

I can hardly wait!
When is the due date?
I hope you're not late!
It's gonna be great!
-Gina Marie Lauchner

PREMATURE BIRTH
(see Hardship)

RAISING HEAD

Yes, this is a nice blanket
But I'm ready for something new.
I think I'll raise my head
And check out the view!
-Crystal Dawn Perry

ROLLING OVER

Forgive my cries.
You are so wise.
You just rolled over.
What a surprise!

After many tries
And whimpering cries
You're viewing the world
With sweeping eyes.
—Aparna Dyer

I'm pushing up, over, and to the side.
I'm rolling over!
Oh, what a ride!
—Dana Roberts Clark

RUNNING

All through the morning
And right up 'til evening
They'll chase and race and run
Then lie their heads
On soft pillows and beds
And dream of tomorrow's fun
Like searching out a secret star
And catching lightning bugs in a jar –
Dreams of a voyage that's just begun.
—Connie Berry

Baby says "bye-bye" and waves to everyone
Short, pudgy legs take off in a run
Down the hallway, fast as can be
Hey, Mommy! You can't catch me!
"I'm gonna get you," she says with delight
Baby starts to squeal and runs with all his might!
—Laura Taylor Mark

Your cherub-like cheeks
So perfectly round
Your tiny bowed lips
Ready to imitate sounds
Watching your zigzag, wobbly run
I know your learning has just begun.
-Crystal Dawn Perry

SANTA CLAUS
(see also Christmas)

Mommy, I don't like this man
With all the white stuff on his face
I thought it might be Daddy
But now my heart is starting to race
Please take me off this guy's lap
Before I really start to cry
I'm outta here; you can't change my mind –
Don't even try!
-Laura Taylor Mark

My sleepy eyes turn bright
When gifts from Santa I see.
Oh, what a sight!
Are ALL these toys for me?
-Crystal Dawn Perry

We go to visit Santa
To drop hints for Christmas Day
But this feeling in my belly
Feels like I want to run away

Uh-oh, he's getting closer, saying
"HO HO HO!"
I don't want to sit on his lap, I said
"NO! NO! NO!"
-Crystal Dawn Perry

SCRAPBOOKING

Mommy's working on her scrapbook
She stays up every night
'Til the wee hours of the morning
Making it just right

Daddy's always taking pictures
Of everything I do
Even when I'm sleeping
I'm in the camera's view

Sometimes, I get embarrassed
By the photos that they show
To anyone who visits
Even people I don't know

Yesterday, the cable guy
Looked at Mommy's book
He thumbed through all the pages
Then he took another look.

I guess I'll keep on smiling
It's really not so bad
To show me off to everyone
Makes Mom and Dad glad.
                    -Brenda Darlene Kijowski

The day that I first smiled
And when I learned to crawl
The time I took my first steps
And didn't even fall

My Mommy keeps a record
Of everything I do
How old I was, the date, the time
The thing that I did new.
                    -Brenda Darlene Kijowski

SIBLING

(see also Brother and Sister)

There's so much to learn
Where shall I begin?
There are things you should know
About this world we live in:
You get your diaper changed
Every time that you wet it.
If we do something cute,
I want all the credit.
You can pick out a book
If I've already read it.
And remember, I was here first--
So don't you forget it!!
    -Gina Marie Lauchner

I'm yours, you are mine
Forever and always 'til
The end of time.

Brother to Sister, Sister to Brother
I will love and protect you
Like no other.
    -Crystal Dawn Perry

Open your eyes little baby,
Please, won't you play with me?
I've been in this world a while now,
Has it been two years or three?
Now, let me tell you something
That you should probably know;
As your big sister, I'm already a pro.
Just notice what I do, just follow my lead
I'll teach you about Daddy's garage,
And we'll help Mommy plant seeds.

I can teach you the art of dance
As you watch me twist and prance
Or else I can teach you to be a singer.
Oh, but I see you've already perfected an art...
The art of wrapping yourself tightly
Around everyone's little finger.
-Crystal Dawn Perry

Little sister, I'm so glad
You've come to play with me.
I'll show you the ropes, share my toys;
I might even serve you a little tea.
I promise to be the best brother,
The best in the world, you'll see!
And when you learn how great I am
I'm sure you'll want to be
Adorable, sweet, perfect-
Just like me!
-Crystal Dawn Perry

SIPPY CUP

This time when they
Hand me the sippy cup
I won't get frustrated
I won't give up
I'll drink all the juice
And I won't spill a drop
I'll hold it the right way
And keep the lid on top
I have to have confidence
I know I can do it
If I believe in myself
And just get out there
And prove it!
-Gina Marie Lauchner

Sippity Sup
I love my sippy cup.
Sippity Gulp
I love my sippy cup.
Sippity Slurp
I love my sippy..."burp!"
-*Crystal Dawn Perry*

SISTER

(see also Sibling)

The bond of sisters
Stands the test of time.
I'm so blessed
That you are mine.
-*Dana Roberts Clark*

My sister is the coolest!
She plays with me,
She holds my hand,
She walks with me,
She helps me stand.
My sister is the best!
-*Carl Joseph Vonnoh, III*

SITTING UP

Today I looked away.
I turned back...you have grown.
Things you couldn't do before,
Now you're doing on your own.
I'm sure it was only yesterday
That you depended on my help.
My, what a smart baby-
Sitting by yourself!
-*Crystal Dawn Perry*

Look what I can do!
I can laugh at peek-a-boo.
I can cry. I can play.
I take naps during the day.
I can eat. I can spit up.
And today I learned to sit up!
-*Crystal Dawn Perry*

SLEEP

Watching you sleep,
Watching you breathe,
A peaceful end to
Another playful day.
More than a glowing sunset,
More than the shining stars,
You, my little one,
Take my breath away.
-*Crystal Dawn Perry*

My baby, my wonder,
You'd sleep through the thunder
Not bothered by any noise.

Neither pouting nor weeping,
You're happily sleeping
And dreaming about all your toys.
-*Aparna Oyer*

Caresses soft and tender
Soothe my little one to sleep
Sweet melodies of comfort
Lull baby fast asleep
Gentle dreams, my cherished child
Tranquil slumber be with you
'Til morning rays are fading
Heaven's night stars from our view.
-*Brenda Darlene Kijowski*

All through the morning
And right up 'til evening
They'll chase and race and run.
Then lie their heads
On soft pillows and beds
And dream of tomorrow's fun
Like searching out a secret star
And catching lightning bugs in a jar-
Dreams of a voyage that's just begun.
                    -Connie Berry

There's nothing quite like
A clean pair of pj's
All soft against my skin.
I'll wear them 'till the very next day,
'Til the morning starts over again.
There's nothing quite like
A clean pair of pj's,
I like these pj's the best to sleep in.
When it's nighttime
it's time to put on my pj's...
Let the sweet dreams begin!
                    -Gina Marie Lauchner

When I've had a day that's taxing,
I hold my baby in my lap.
Nothing could ever be as relaxing
As both of us taking a nap.
                    -Aparna Dyer

Now I lay me down to sleep
And say a little prayer.
I hope to God that I wake up
With a head of hair.

I don't care if it is straight
And doesn't have any curl.
I just want everyone to know
That I really am a girl!
                    -Aparna Dyer

Eyelashes resting on pouty cheeks
Ten precious toes on two precious feet
From head to toe, from toe to head
The world's most precious angel
Lies sleeping in your bed.
-Crystal Dawn Perry

SMILE

You are an undeniable beauty,
The world warmed by your radiance.
Your eyes sparkle and intrigue.
Your smile brightens and enchants.
Watching your beauty, inside and out
I say, "Thank you, Dear Angel,
You have taught my soul to dance."
-Crystal Dawn Perry

A toothless mouth
Forms Daddy's smile
A show of love
Sweet and infantile

No reason needed except
Your face in view
You smile at me,
I smile at you!
-Brenda Darlene Kijowski

Have you heard the platitude
That life is mainly attitude?
With the lift of your chin
And your sneakiest grin
Attitude is what you exude!
-Aparna Dyer

The day that I first smiled
And when I learned to crawl
The time I took my first steps
And didn't even fall

My Mommy keeps a record
Of everything I do
How old I was, the date, the time
The thing that I did new.
   -Brenda Darlene Kijowski

I used to listen to the weather,
But lately I don't seem to care.
Sunshine and rain no longer matter,
Except in the expression you wear.

When raindrops dare to dampen
The sweet windows of your soul,
Washing away your tender tears
Is my most important goal.

And when the sunshine reappears
In your charming, disarming smile,
I know I'll save that warming image,
In my eternal memory file.
   -Aparna Dyer

SON

Empty out those pockets, Son
The ones you filled with dreams
This morning, they were empty
Now they're bursting at the seams

What have you found to save today?
What magic can you share?
Tell Mommy what you dreamed about
The what and when and where

What treasures have you gathered, Son?
Collected on your way
To all those special places
You travel in a day

Did you catch a speedy rocket
To a distant shiny star
And pocket rocks when leaving
To keep as your memoirs

Did you hike into the mountains
And chance to meet a bear
Then use your trusty water gun
To give that bear a scare

Did you hop a railroad car in town
Then travel far away
And bring that pretty flower back
To give to me today

Empty out your pockets, Son
They're bursting at the seams
And speak of your adventures, dear
Tell Mommy of your dreams.
          -Brenda Darlene Kijowski

I can hardly remember the days
Before you were my sunshine.
I feel like I have always loved you,
Like you have always been mine.

Now my days are brighter from
Your smiles and moments at play.
You are my life's shining star...
The 'son' that brightens my day.
          -Crystal Dawn Perry

Boys will be boys
They always say
But boys fight rough
Whenever they play.

Boys will be boys
That's a well-known rule.
When boys play tough
They think they are cool.
-Gina Marie Lauchner

He's a little touch of Heaven
Sent down from above.
He's filled our lives with happiness
And our hearts full of love.
-Dana Roberts Clark

Rough and tumble, climbing trees,
Cuts, scrapes, bandaged skinned knees.

Dump trucks, fire engines, shiny red cars,
Bugs, worms, grass and dirt in a jar.

Mischievous twinkle in their bright eyes,
Little all-stars and one of the guys!
-Laura Taylor Mark

SPECIAL NEEDS
(see Hardship)

ST. PATRICK'S DAY

Let me dress you up in green
And I'll carry you on my arm.
You can be my little leprechaun
You're already my lucky charm.
-Crystal Dawn Perry

What is up with all the green?
Is this what happens on March 17?
I don't even know my colors that well
But everything is green; that I can tell.
Even that little guy who's smaller than me
A leprechaun...how does he stay so green?
Just in case the colors fade away
I'll have my green crayon ready...
Just for today!
-*Gina Marie Lauchner*

STANDING / PULLING UP

Up, up, and not quite away
I just learned to stand today
Soon I'll be able to run and play
For now, I'll just stand here and sway.
-*Crystal Dawn Perry*

Look what I did! Look at me!
Quick! Snap a picture
Before I fall to my knees –
I've pulled myself up
To see what I can see!
-*Crystal Dawn Perry*

My sister is the coolest!
She plays with me,
She holds my hand,
She walks with me,
She helps me stand.
My sister is the best!
-*Carl Joseph Vonnoh, III*

Pulling up, holding on
It's time to explore.

Maybe I'll find a treasure –
Oh, boy! I have scored!

A marker, a pen, a nearly full cup
I wonder if this will pour?

Cruising furniture is an adventure.
I'm ready to venture more!
-*Crystal Dawn Perry*

STAY - AT - HOME   MOTHER

Stay at home mom
That's what they say
But it seems that I must
Leave nearly every day
You say, "So what?
Your life can't be beat?"
Well, just like you,
I dread the car seats.
In addition to that
The kids have bad days
But there is no escape,
No getting away.
Spills, fights and smashes,
Make me want to pull out my hair.
I know your job has this effect too
But my job is always there.
I don't always get a shower and
The beds aren't always made
But when I tuck them in at night, I admit,
These are days I wouldn't trade.
-*Crystal Dawn Perry*

STEP - PARENT / STEP - SIBLING

Mom's kids and Dad's kids
Together we are the best
As step brothers and step sisters
We are a step above the rest!
-Crystal Dawn Perry

When we were alone,
You stepped in.
When we were down,
You stepped up.
You know when to take charge
Or when to step down.
You are a step above the rest...
The best step-parent around.
-Crystal Dawn Perry

One of us, I'm proud to be
He, she, we, them and me,
This awesome family
Blended perfectly.
-Crystal Dawn Perry

STUFFED ANIMAL / TEDDY BEAR

I have a very precious friend
As special as can be
Nobody else is quite like him
And I should know, you see

I tell him all my secrets
He listens very well
To all my troubles, hopes and dreams
And never, never tells.

I have a very special friend
For me, he's always there.
I hold him tight when feeling blue
He is my Teddy Bear.
-Brenda Darlene Kijowski

I have an extra special friend
Who is always here for me
To listen to my troubles
And shoo away every worry.

Most children have a teddy bear
Who listens to their fears
But I prefer another friend
To wash away my tears.

He doesn't miss a single word
He hears me loud and clear
Even when I whisper soft
Because he is all ears.

I call him Bunny Rarebit
He is earmarked for stardom
'Cause he listens even better
Than any bunny, you've heard of.
-Brenda Darlene Kijowski

I always have fun but
If I have to compare
The times I like best
Are the times that I share
Creating loving memories
With my teddy bear.
-Crystal Dawn Perry

SWING

When I'm swinging in the swing
I'm free as a bird
Like a bird on a swinging lap
I'm a bird on a swing
Flying forward and back
I'm like a bird...
A bird taking a nap.
-Gina Marie Lauchner

Back and forth, forth and back
Sounds of crying give way
To the sound of 'clickity-clack'

Thanks to the Lord up above
For sending peace to all
With this swing that is loved.

-Crystal Dawn Perry

Back and forth, pace the floor, rocking in a swing
Fussy babies test our love when they begin to "sing"
When they're done crying and finally go to sleep
Weary parents are thankful
This is one habit that baby doesn't keep!

-Laura Taylor Mark

TALKING

The things you say
As you learn to speak
Change every day
Even more so each week
The language is not easy
But you continue to seek
New words to turn
Upside down in your cheeks.

-Gina Marie Lauchner

Abba, gaba, hada, raba,
Daba, baba, do.
I know sweetheart,
I love you too!

-Dana Roberts Clark

Bursts of sound become ideas
As babe begins to babble
And first words soon are spoken
Ma Ma, Da Da, she does ramble.

-Brenda Darlene Kijowski

Your cherub-like cheeks
So perfectly round
Your tiny bowed lips
Ready to imitate sounds
Watching your zigzag, wobbly run
I know your learning has just begun.
    -Crystal Dawn Perry

TEETH / TEETHING

With all the drooling, chewing
And pain that you were in
It's so nice to see that teeth
Have replaced that gummy grin!
    -Laura Taylor Mark

After all the drooling,
The fussing and the pain,
I deserve to get more
Than this tiny tooth
That I have gained!
    -Crystal Dawn Perry

My tooth! My tooth!
I just got my first tooth!
And though this is neat,
I feel quite uncouth
...with only one tooth.
    -Carl Joseph Vonnoh, DDD

I used to hold your bottle
Now you hold it by yourself.
You've just begun to toddle
And pull your toys off the shelf.

We hardly use your stroller
'Cause you're walking on your own.
You've grown your first molar;
You're even talking on the phone.

It's only been a year
And look at all that you can do.
I wipe away a tear
As I imagine you at two.
    —Aparna Dyer

THANKSGIVING

Recognizing family, friends,
And enough blessings to share,
A Thanksgiving feast
With food to spare.

Rich in tradition,
How blessed are we.
Our family shares this day
Making memories.
    —Crystal Dawn Perry

A time for thanks
A time to pray
For our many blessings
This Thanksgiving Day.
    —Crystal Dawn Perry

TODDLER
(see also Child/Children)

The life of a toddler is not as easy as it seems
There are issues such as forgotten diapers, sharing,
And being the target of brother's screams.
Everyday there are stumped toes, wild emotions,
And the occasional skinned knee,
Ladies in the stores commenting on my hair bow
Then asking, "How old is HE?"
Now that I've explained this
I'm sure that you can see

Why a girl must have her blankie
In desperate times such as these.
      -Crystal Dawn Perry

[substitute:]
Ladies in the stores commenting on my baseball cap
Then asking, "How old is SHE?"
Now that I've explained this
I'm sure you can see
Why a boy must have his [favorite object]
In desperate times such as these.

I used to hold your bottle
Now you hold it by yourself.
You've just begun to toddle
And pull your toys off the shelf.

We hardly use your stroller
'Cause you're walking on your own.
You've grown your first molar;
You're even talking on the phone.

It's only been a year
And look at all that you can do.
I wipe away a tear
As I imagine you at two.
      -Aparna Dyer

I was pregnant then I blinked my eyes...
And I held you in my arms.
I brought you home then I blinked my eyes...
Your first smile showed me your charms.
I watched you crawl then I blinked my eyes...
And you were running down the hall.
You're growing so fast; forgive my cries.
I was pregnant then I blinked my eyes.
      -Dana Roberts Clark

Your cherub-like cheeks
So perfectly round
Your tiny bowed lips
Ready to imitate sounds
Watching your zigzag, wobbly run
I know your learning has just begun.
-Crystal Dawn Perry

Home from the hospital, your first night here
As I caressed your face and held you near
I noticed that in my palm, I could hold your tiny feet.
This must have been the night that I fell asleep.

When I awoke, I heard you cry for me.
Here is a toddler. Where is my baby?
Has this much time really passed
Or are you growing exceedingly fast?

As I think of the first days again
Certainly, the days seem a dream
Yesterday, you were my heart's glisten.
Today, my heart's lively gleam.
-Crystal Dawn Perry

TOILET TRAINING

I am toilet training
I just made a mad dash!
I'll really miss those diapers
But I won't miss diaper rash!
-Aparna Oyer

I'm so tired. I'm so weary.
Who picked me up and called me "Deary"?
Who sat me on that ol' cold pot
And told me to, when I could not?
I'm not sure but I think it was my mommy.
Mommy! Mommy! I'm through!
-Unknown

Potty training
Is very straining
I hit the seat
Even though I'm aiming!
-Carl Joseph Vonnoh, III

Mommy has opened the sink's tap
To make it sound like rain.
I think I'll just take a nap
As I toilet train.
-Aparna Dyer

TOYS

(see also: Balls, Blocks, Doll, and
Stuffed Animal / Teddy Bear)

The life of a toddler is not as easy as it seems
There are issues such as forgotten diapers, sharing,
And being the target of brother's screams.
Everyday there are stumped toes, wild emotions,
And the occasional skinned knee,
Ladies in the stores commenting on my hair bow
Then asking, "How old is HE?"
Now that I've explained this
I'm sure you can see
Why a girl must have her favorite toy
In desperate times such as these.
-Crystal Dawn Perry

[substitute:]
Ladies in the stores commenting on my baseball cap
Then asking, "How old is SHE?"
Now that I've explained this
I'm sure you can see
Why a boy must have his [favorite object]
In desperate times such as these.

Upside down, turn around,
Spinning round and round,
Make a face, play pat-a-cake,
Tumble to the ground

Building blocks, wind-up clocks,
Soft toys on a blankie,
Pretty soon it's naptime for
A very tired Mommy!
  —*Laura Taylor Mark*

Watching you play,
I see the wonder in your eyes.
I see more than fun for you.
I see you learning every day.
  —*Crystal Dawn Perry*

I used to hold your bottle
Now you hold it by yourself.
You've just begun to toddle
And pull your toys off the shelf.

We hardly use your stroller
'Cause you're walking on your own.
You've grown your first molar;
You're even talking on the phone.

It's only been a year
And look at all that you can do.
I wipe away a tear
As I imagine you at two.
  —*Aparna Dyer*

My sister is the coolest!
She plays with me,
She holds my hand,
She walks with me,
She helps me stand.
My sister is the best!
  —*Carl Joseph Vonnoh, DDD*

My beautiful daughter
I'm proud that your spirit soars
As you find pleasure in life, in toys,
And in the people you adore.

You have a love for discovery;
I hope your wishes will be explored.
On this journey of life, remember-
You couldn't be loved any more.
-Crystal Dawn Perry

When Daddy throws me in the air,
It gives me such an awful scare.
When I come down, he catches me.
I want to cry, but I say, "wheee!"
-Laura Taylor Mark

Learning to play
Learning to share
Making first friends
And learning to care
Playdates with children
You have come to adore
Each day spent together
Leaves them loving you more.
-Crystal Dawn Perry

TRADITION

Memories made; moving forward
Days remembered; looking back
Togetherness, sharing, laughter,
Looking forward to coming back.
-Crystal Dawn Perry

Treasured times
Repeated
Again & again
Deep-rooted
In
Tradition
Invariably
Of
Notation
-Crystal Dawn Perry

Rich in tradition
How blessed are we
That we can share this day
Making memories.
-Crystal Dawn Perry

TRAVEL / VACATION

Baby needs so many things
Just to get through the day
By the time I'm packed and ready to go
Home is where I want to stay!
-Laura Taylor Mark

Your first day at the beach
Was such a sandy treat
From your diapered little bottom
To your precious little feet
I found sand on you in places
I didn't know you had
No wonder you had such fun
Thinking you were being bad!
-Laura Taylor Mark

Diapers, wipees, and food
Blankets, bibs and toys for play
We must take half our home
To the place that we will stay.

Pack and pack some more.
Oh, there is so much to take;
Packed tightly with lots of love
Into these memories we will make.
-*Crystal Dawn Perry*

Memories made; moving forward
Days remembered; looking back
Togetherness, sharing, laughter,
Looking forward to coming back.
-*Crystal Dawn Perry*

TROUBLE

Look at the pretty picture, Mommy
I made it just for you.
Mommy, don't look at me that way
The wall looks nice in blue.
-*Laura Taylor Mark*

What is it about trouble
That attracts the brightest and best?
Maybe it just follows us
Maybe it is a test.
Maybe it is hard
To turn the other way
When trouble comes a-knockin'
And wants us to go play.
-*Gina Marie Lauchner*

ULTRASOUND

Soft flutter of feeling
Those moments before birth
The knowing of you
The beginning of you
So close to the heart of me
A first glimpse
A chance to see
In a tiny little image
Of shadow and light –
Small curves and features
Each so uniquely you
Framed and treasured those long weeks
Before our eyes first met and
I could clearly see each curled lash
And touch each tiny toenail
And breathe your precious scent
And know just how perfect you truly are.

-Connie Berry

I heard the sound of your heart,
And my own heart skipped a beat.
There you were, moving around,
In your safe and quiet retreat.

I think I saw your button nose,
Or was that your right ear?
Either way, I know that I
Will hold you near and dear.

I want to tickle those little feet,
That kick me night and day
I want to hear you coo and cry
I want to watch you play.

A picture may be worth
A thousand words or more,
But I just can't wait to hold
The little baby I adore.

-Aparna Dyer

Today is the day!
Oh, what a joy!
We're going to find out
If you're a girl or a boy!

The doctor can't tell
If you're a girl or a fellow
I guess we'll play it safe
And paint the nursery yellow.

I'm overjoyed to hear you're healthy
But hear your Mommy beg –
Please turn this way a little
And uncross your little legs!
-Crystal Dawn Perry

UNCLE

"I'll be a monkey's uncle!"
We've all heard it said,
It leaves me warm and fuzzy
Yet scratching my head.

What could it be that
A monkey's uncle would do?
Bring me bananas or
Visit me at the zoo?

He could lift me up
So I could swing from a tree
I could check him for bugs
And he could check me

If you are a monkey's uncle
That monkey is very lucky
And there's one thing for sure,
I'm glad that monkey is me!
-Crystal Dawn Perry

VALENTINE'S DAY

(see also Love)

They make such a big deal
About Valentine's Day.
Kissing and hugging?
Red and pink? No way!

All that mushy, love-y stuff
What's the big deal?
Enough is enough!

Well, maybe I wouldn't mind
A candy or two
I'll guess I'll be your Valentine
If you'll be mine too!
-Gina Marie Lauchner

You excite my heart
With the way you play.
You warm my heart
With the babbling you say.
You hold my heart
Forever and always.
Please be mine
On this Valentine's Day!
-Crystal Dawn Perry

WALKING

Take my hand, if but for a moment
To walk the path together
And share and laugh and grow a little
As I show this world to you.
Days will pass and months will fade
And soon you'll walk on your own
And take those steps – those first few steps
That will lead to a life of your own.
I'll stand and watch right here beside you
Each triumph, smile and lesson learned
And keep in my a heart a memory sweet
Of these tiny fingers clasped 'round mine
As you toddled forward for the very first time.
-Connie Berry

Today, I'm walking to you
With a stagger and a sway.
Take my hand. Be my guide.
I'm just beginning on my way.

Please know that as my steps get firm
Today is a memory that will fade.
I need your continued support through life
The way I feel it today.

One day I'll follow your footsteps
As they guide me along the way.
You'll hold my heart as you held my hand
Remember, you'll be my guide always.
-Crystal Dawn Perry

I'm learning how to walk
And balance on my feet
Pretty soon I'll be running
And skipping down the street
Pretty soon I'll be jumping
And hopping up and down
But for now I should just try
Keeping my feet on the ground.
-Gina Marie Lauchner

Ten tiny toes on
Two softly padded feet
Symbols of innocence ...
What will they carry you to meet?
-Crystal Dawn Perry

I used to hold your bottle
Now you hold it by yourself.
You've just begun to toddle
And pull your toys off the shelf.

We hardly use your stroller
'Cause you're walking on your own.
You've grown your first molar;
You're even talking on the phone.

It's only been a year
And look at all that you can do.
I wipe away a tear
As I imagine you at two.
-Aparna Dyer

My baby brother is learning to walk
But he has trouble getting around
He stands up by holding onto things
Then lets go and falls to the ground

When he falls down, he lands with a thump
It's then that he starts bawling
I think I'd give up if it hurt so much
And maybe just stick to crawling.
-John Beith

The day that I first smiled
And when I learned to crawl
The time I took my first steps
And didn't even fall

My Mommy keeps a record
Of everything I do
How old I was, the date, the time
The thing that I did new.
-Brenda Darlene Kijowski

There is no magic day
No way for you to know
No time to take a picture
For you to proudly show
But the memory is forever
Engraved in your mind
When one shaking little leg
Leaves the other leg behind.
-Dana Roberts Clark

WORKING MOTHER

Finances seem to limit
My choice at home to stay
So I trust my precious package
To grandparents through the day.
-Brenda Darlene Kijowski

Love and joy reach out to me
As I enter through the door
Tiny arms stretching to hug me
Wrapping 'round my neck once more

It is hard to leave my child
In another person's care
But when she runs to meet me
Her love, I know I share

Her understanding nature
Makes my working less a chore
And each night when I return to here
My heart, she does restore.
-Brenda Darlene Kijowski

Poems

Poems

Poems

Quotes, Crafty Sayings and Scriptures

ADOPTION

Biology is the least of what makes someone a mother.
-Oprah Winfrey

Each dawn holds a new hope for a new plan,
making the start of each day the start of a new life.
-Gina Blair

God meets our needs in unexpected ways.
-Janette Oke

The bond that links your true family is not one of blood,
but of respect and joy in each other's life.
-Richard Bach

It is not flesh and blood but the heart
which makes us fathers and sons.
-Schiller

Adoption is when a child grew in
its mommy's heart instead of her tummy.
-Unknown

The family that you come from isn't as
important as the family you're going to have.
-Ring Lardner

Small child – once you were a hope, a dream.
Now you are a reality. Changing all that is to come...
A love to hold our hearts forever.
-Charlotte Gray

Our ties seem so deep, coming from some faraway
dark womblike place, that they can be no different
nor less than those of the biological parent.
-Nan Bauer Maglin

Thou art my Son, this day have I begotten thee?
And again, I will be to him a Father, and he shall be to me a Son.

Hebrews 1:5 (KJV)

ATTITUDE

If you can't change your fate, change your attitude.

-Amy Tan

He that can have patience can have what he will.

-Benjamin Franklin

Mad, bad, and dangerous to know.

-Lady Caroline Lamb

I am as bad as the worst,

but Thank God, I am as good as the best.

-Walt Whitman

This free-will business is a bit terrifying anyway.
It's almost pleasanter to obey, and make the most of it.

-Ugo Betti

I am better than my reputation.

-Friedrich von Schiller

BABY

(see also Birth/Newborn and Child/Children)

A baby is a bit of stardust
blown from the hand of God!

God's littlest lambs are the most precious of His flock.

-Lisa R. Walker

Flowers are words which even a baby can understand.
-Arthur C. Coxe

Baby's fishing for a dream, Fishing near and far,
His line a silver moonbeam, His bait a silver star.
-Alice C.D. Riley

Life is the first gift,
Love is the second and
Understanding the third.
-Marge Piercy

Oh, the places you'll go!
-Dr. Seuss

Small child – once you were a hope, a dream.
Now you are a reality. Changing all that is to come...
A love to hold our hearts forever.
-Charlotte Gray

There is no other closeness in human life like the closeness betwee
a mother and her baby: chronologically, physically, and
spiritually,they are just a few heartbeats away from
being the same person.
-Susan Cheever

A baby is always more trouble than you thought
– and more wonderful.
-Charles Osgood

A baby is God's opinion that the world should go on.
-Carl Sandburg

Having a baby is like falling in love again,
both with your husband and your child.
-Tina Brown

Before you were born, I thought you were perfect;
after you were born, I knew you were.
-Crystal Dawn Perry

The infant is music itself.
-Hazrat Onayat Khan

Other things change us,
but we start and end with the family.
-Anthony Brandt

It is not a slight thing when they,
who are so fresh from God, love us.
-Charles Dickens

A baby costs more than anything else
on earth...your love, your life.
-Helen Thomson

A lovely being, scarcely formed or molded,
a rose with all its sweetest leaves yet folded.
-Lord Byron

Babies are such a nice way to start people.
-Don Herold

When you love someone, all your saved-up wishes start coming out.
-Elizabeth Bowen

Where there is great love, there are always miracles.
Willa Cather

From small beginnings come great things.
-Proverb

All of God's creatures are held in the hands of His kindness.
Janet Weaver

God specializes in things fresh and firsthand.
His plans for you this year may outshine those of the past;
He's preparing to fill your days with reasons to give Him praise.
Joni Eareckson Tada

And God saw everything that He had made,
and, behold, it was very good.

Genesis 1:31

Thanks be to God for His
indescribable gift!

2 Corinthians 9:15 (NIV)

BABY SHOWER

The real secret of happiness is not what you give or receive;
it's what you share.

May no gift be too small to give nor too simple to receive,
which is wrapped in thoughtfulness and tied with love.

-L. O. Baird

A friend is a gift you give yourself.

-Robert Louis Stevenson

Each day comes bearing its own gifts. Untie the ribbons.

-Ruth Ann Schabacker

To have a friend is to have one of the sweetest gifts that life can
bring.

-Amy Robertson Brown

Change always comes bearing gifts.

-Price Pritchett

Yesterday is history. Tomorrow is a mystery. And today?
Today is a gift. That's why we call it the present.

-Babatunde Olatunji

There shall be showers of blessing.

Ezekiel 34:26 (KJV)

BABYSITTER

Being constantly with the children was like wearing a pair
of shoes that were expensive and too small. She couldn't
bear to throw them out, but they gave her blisters.
-Beryl Bainbridge

One hour with a child is like a ten-mile run.
-Joan Benoit Samuelson

Few things help an individual more
than to place responsibility upon him,
and to let him know that you trust him.
-Booker T. Washington

Few delights can equal the mere presence
of one whom we trust utterly.
-George MacDonald

I figure if the kids are alive at the end of the day, I've done my job.
-Roseanne Barr

Responsibility: A detachable burden easily shifted to the
shoulders of God, Fate, Fortune, Luck or one's neighbor. In
the days of astrology, it was customary
to unload it upon a star.
-Ambrose Bierce

Leaving a child for the first time feels as though we are
leaving a small piece of our heart - the place in our heart where we
stored all of our together times. Immediately,
we feel the need to restore it; desperately hoping
that piece of our heart cannot be erased.
-Crystal Dawn Perry

BALLS

Life's a ball when you're having fun.
To give yourself the best possible chance of playing
to your potential, you must prepare for
every eventuality.
That means practice.
-Seve Ballesteros

It is in games that many men discover their paradise.
-Robert Lynd

BATH

If children are the ones who take the baths,
why are moms the ones who get soaking wet?

A newborn's first experience in bath water...how nostalgic.
-Crystal Dawn Perry

Everything is miraculous.
It is miraculous that one does not melt in one's bath.
-Pablo Picasso

I believe in getting into hot water; it keeps you clean.
-G.K. Chesterton

What soap is for the body, tears are for the soul.
-Jewish Proverb

Even when freshly washed and relieved of all obvious confections,
children tend to be sticky.
-Fran Lebowitz

BEAUTY

Thin people are beautiful
but fat people are adorable.
-Jackie Gleason

We find delight in the beauty and happiness of children
that makes the heart too big for the body.
-R.W. Emerson

A heart in love with beauty never grows old.
-Turkish proverb

God's fingers can touch nothing but to mold it into loveliness.
-George MacDonald

The simple beauty of a toddler is greater
than every artistic masterpiece combined.
-Carl Joseph Vonnoh, OOO

A thing of beauty is a joy forever.
Its loveliness increases; it will never pass into nothingness.
-John Keats

Beauty is not caused. It is.
-Emily Dickinson

And all the loveliest things there be come simply, so it seems to me.
-Edna St. Vincent Millay

In all ranks of life, the human heart yearns for the beautiful;
and the beautiful things that God makes are His gift to all alike.
-Harriet Beecher Stowe

Though we travel the world over to find the beautiful,
we must carry it with us or we find it not.
-Ralph Waldo Emerson

BIRTH / NEWBORN
(see also Baby)

If it were going to be easy to raise kids,
it wouldn't have started with something called labor.

When they placed you in my arms, you slipped into my heart.

The most amazing moment was when he was handed to me, in
his little blanket, and looked at me with his huge blue eyes.
-Margaret Drabble

I think my life began with waking up and loving mother's face.
-George Eliot

The very pink of perfection.
-Oliver Goldsmith

It is strangely miraculous to see and to hold a living being
formed within oneself and issued forth from oneself.
-Simone de Beauvoir

Please forgive me for smiling when I first heard your cry.
It was the most beautiful pitiful sound I had ever heard.
-Crystal Dawn Perry

There was a star danced, and under that was I born.
-William Shakespeare

Nothing is more than this day.
-Goethe

Every child born into the world is a new thought of God,
an ever-fresh and radiant possibility.
-Kate Douglas Wiggin

A new baby is like the beginning of all things –
wonder, hope, a dream of possibilities.
-Eda J. Le Shan

Before you were conceived, I wanted you.
Before you were born, I loved you.
Before you were here for an hour, I would die for you.
This is the miracle of life.
-Maureen Hawkins

Of all the things that lighten suffering earth,
what joy is welcomed like a new-born child?
-Caroline Norton

When a child is born, so is a grandmother.
-Italian proverb

I looked at this tiny, perfect creature and it was as though a light
switch had been turned on. A great rush of love flooded out of me.
-Madeleine L'Engle

Suddenly she was here. And I was no longer pregnant; I was a
mother.
I never believed in miracles before.
-Ellen Greene

When a woman puts her finger for the first time into the
tiny hand of her baby and feels that helpless clutch
which tightens her very heartstrings, she is
born again with the newborn child.
-Kate Douglas Wiggin

Nobody said giving birth is easy,
but there's no other way to get the job done.
-Ivana Trump

Death and taxes and childbirth.
There's never any convenient time for any of them.
-Margaret Mitchell

The night you were born, I ceased being my father's boy and became
my son's father. That night I began a new life.
-*Henry Gregor Felson*

I will praise thee; for I am fearfully and wonderfully made:
marvelous are thy works.
Psalm 139:14 (KJV)

Thanks be to God for His indescribable gift!
2Corinthians 9:15 (NIV)

BIRTHDAY

Do not be sad that the first year has passed so quickly
but rejoice that it was your experience.
-*Crystal Dawn Perry*

All kids are gifted:
Some just open their packages earlier than others.
-*Michael Carr*

Yesterday is history. Tomorrow is a mystery. And today?
Today is a gift. That's why we call it the present.
-*Babatunde Olatunji*

Each day comes bearing its own gifts. Untie the ribbons.
-*Ruth Ann Schubacker*

When a man is wrapped up in himself, he makes a pretty small
package.
-*John Ruskin*

We turn not older with the years, but newer every day.
-*Emily Dickinson*

He who is of a calm and happy nature
will hardly feel the pressure of age.
-*Plato*

Because time itself is like a spiral, something special happens on your birthday each year: the same energy that God invested in you at birth is present once again.
-*Menachem Mendel Schneerson*

God specializes in things fresh and firsthand.
His plans for you this year may outshine those of the past;
He's preparing to fill your days with reasons to give Him praise.
-*Joni Eareckson Tada*

Grow old along with me! The best is yet to be.
-*Robert Browning*

BIRTH DEFECT
(*see Hardship*)

BIRTHMARK

A birthmark is God's fingerprint, left to remind us He was here first.
-*Crystal Dawn Perry*

BLANKET

Life is like a blanket too short. You pull it up, and your toes rebel.
You yank it down, and shivers meander about your shoulder;
but cheerful folks manage to draw their knees up
and pass a very comfortable night.
-*Marion Howard*

A security blanket gives warmth, not because it is draped over the child, but because it is quilted with the imagery of everything loved...
home, favorite toys, favorite people.
-*Crystal Dawn Perry*

Vice goes a long toward making life bearable.
A little vice now and then is relished by the best of men.
-*Finley Peter Dunne*

The best security blanket a child can have is parents
who respect each other.
-Jan Blaustone

Think what a better world it would be if we all,
the whole world, had cookies and milk
about three o'clock every afternoon and then
lay down on our blankets for a nap.
-Barbara Jordan

Does it seem impossible that the child will grow up?
That the bashful smile will become a bold expression...
that a briefcase will replace the blue security blanket?
-Ann Beattie

BLOCKS

If you build it, they will come.

Our todays and yesterdays are the blocks with which we build.
-Henry Wadsworth Longfellow

Building blocks, like learning to stand...
the higher you get, the harder the fall.
-Crystal Dawn Perry

BOOK

A good book has no ending.
-R.D. Cumming

In the book of life, the answers aren't in the back.
-Charles Schultz, Charlie Brown

I would be most content if my children grew up to be the kind of
people who think decorating consists mostly of building
enough bookshelves.
-Anna Quindlen

Judicious mothers will always keep in mind that they are the
first book read, and the last put aside in every child's library.
-C. Lenox Remond

BOTTLE

They speak of my drinking,
but never think of my thirst.
-Scottish Proverb

Think what a better world it would be if we all,
the whole world, had cookies and milk
about three o'clock every afternoon and then
lay down on our blankets for a nap.
-Barbara Jordan

My "formula" for living is quite simple.
I get up in the morning and I go to bed at night.
In between, I occupy myself as best I can.
-Cary Grant

A child is fed with milk and praise.
-Mary Lamb

He is like many other geniuses,
a greater friend to the bottle than the bottle is to him.
-William Lyon Mackenzie

He who drinks a little too much drinks much too much.
-Old Saying

...a man hath no better thing under the sun,
than to eat, and to drink, and to be merry.
Ecclesiastes 8:15 (KJV)

BOYS
(see Son)

BREAST FEEDING

Just as breast milk cannot be duplicated, neither can a mother.
-Sally Shaywitz

A babe at the breast is as much pleasure as the bearing is pain.
-Marion Zimmer Bradley

A child is fed with milk and praise.
-Mary Lamb

What greater thing is there for human souls
than to feel that they are joined for life –
to be with each other in silent unspeakable memories.
-George Eliot

To love the tender heart hath ever fled,
as on its mother's breast the infant throw its sobbing face,
and there in sleep forgets its woe.
-Mary Tighe

BROTHER

A brother is a friend given by Nature.
-Legouve

A new brother brings the potential for future fights and
shared trouble...and all of the excitement that comes with it.
-Crystal Dawn Perry

Brothers may fight;
but woe betides the one who dares to come between them!
-Carl Joseph Vonnoh, ODO

Big Brother is watching you.
-George Orwell

Am I my brother's keeper?
Genesis 4:9 (KJV)

CAT / KITTEN

What feeling is so nice as a child's hand in yours?
So small, so soft and warm,
like a kitten huddling in the shelter of your clasp.
-Marjorie Holmes

There is something about the presence of a cat...
that seems to take the bite out of being alone.
-Louis J. Camuti

When I play with my cat, who knows if I am not
a pastime to her more than she is to me?
-Montaigne

CHILD / CHILDREN
(see also Baby, Everyday and Toddler)

Blessed are the children...for theirs is a world of wonder.

A child's love is like the dawn unfolding...bright, new and full of hope.

A mother's children are portraits of herself.

Looking into your wide eyes, I can see your trust, your intrigue,
and your thirst for knowledge; and I can only hope that I can fulfill
your life with these things, as you fulfill my life simply by being you.
-Crystal Dawn Perry

Children are the keys of paradise.
-Richard Stoddard-

Every child comes with the message that God is not yet discouraged
-*Rabindranath Tagore*

A child is the greatest poem ever known.
-*Christopher Morley*

While we try to teach our children all about life,
our children teach us what life is all about.
-*Angel Schwindt*

It is not a slight thing when they, who are so fresh from God, love us
-*Charles Dickens*

Youth is, after all, just a moment...but it is the moment,
the spark that you always carry in your heart.
-*Raisa Gorbechev*

You have a unique message to deliver, a unique song to sing,
a unique act of love to bestow. This message, this song, and this act
of love have been entrusted exclusively to the one and only you.
-*John Powell*

Blessed be childhood, which brings down something of Heaven into
the midst of our rough earthiness.
-*Henri Frederic Amiel*

When you're young, the silliest notions
seem the greatest achievements.
-*Pearl Bailey*

A child's spirit is like a child... you can never catch it by running
after it; you must stand still, and for love, it will soon itself come
back.
-*A. Miller*

Children are the hands by which we take hold of Heaven.
-*Henry Ward Beecher*

Children are God's apostles, day by day,
sent forth to preach of love, and hope, and peace.
-*James Russell Lowell*

The sight of you...is as necessary for me
as is the sun for the spring flowers.
-*Marguerite of Valois*

Children in a family are like flowers in a bouquet:
there's always one determined to face in an opposite direction
from the way the arranger desires.
-*Marcelene Cox*

The soul is healed by being with children.
-*Fyodor Dostoevsky*

Children are poor men's riches.
-*English Proverb*

Give a little love to a child and you get a great deal back.
J. Ruskin

The little child, when it sees a star sparkle,
stretches out its dimpled arms; it wants that star.
To want a star is the beautiful insanity of the young.
-*Countess de Gasparin*

Children are the living messages we send to a time we will not see.
John H. Whitehead

Lo, children are an heritage of the Lord:
and the fruit of the womb is his reward.
Psalms 127:3 (KJV)

For where your treasure is, there will your heart be also.
Matthew 1:21 (NIV)

CHRISTENING / DEDICATION

God's greatest creation is not the flung stars or the gorged canyons;
it's His eternal plan to reach His children.
-Max Lucado

The dedicated life is the life worth living.
-Annie Dilliard

God's littlest lambs are the most precious of his flock.
-Lisa R. Walker

Nothing is more than this day.
-Goethe

And he took the children in his arms,
put his hands on them and blessed them.
Mark 10:16 (NIV)

Whoever welcomes one of these little children in my name welcomes
me; and whoever welcomes me does not welcome me
but the one who sent me.
Mark 9:37 (NIV)

CHRISTMAS
(see also Santa Claus)

The magical dust of Christmas glittered on the cheeks of humanity
ever so briefly, reminding us of what is worth having and
what we were intended to be.
-Max Lucado

Christmas is the day that holds all time together.
-Alexander Smith

Christmas, my child, is love in action...
Every time we love, every time we give, it's Christmas.
-Dale Evans Rogers

When a man is wrapped up in himself, he makes a pretty small
package.
-John Ruskin

It is good to be children sometimes, and never better than at
Christmas, when its mighty founder was a child himself.
-Charles Dickens

Each day comes bearing its own gifts. Untie the ribbons.
-Ruth Ann Schubacker

All kids are gifted;
some just open their packages earlier than others.
-Michael Carr

For unto us a child is born, unto us a son is given.
Isaiah 9:1 (KJV)

Glory to God in the highest, and on earth peace, good will toward
men.
St. Luke 2:14 (KJV)

C O L O R I N G

The walls are the publishers of the poor.
-Eduardo Galeano

The only artists for whom I would make way are children. For me,
the paintings of children belong side by side with the works of the
masters.
-Henry Miller

Every child is an artist.
The problem is how to remain an artist once he grows up.
-Pablo Picasso

Imagination is more important than knowledge.
-*Albert Einstein*

COMING HOME

Home is a place where the small are great and the great are small.

From quiet homes and first beginnings out to the undiscovered ends...
-*Hilaire Belloc*

Where is home? Home is where the heart can laugh without shyness
Home is where the heart's tears can dry at the their own pace.
-*Vernon G. Baker*

Home is the one place in all this world
where hearts are sure of each other.
-*Frederick W. Robertson*

Home is a place not only of strong affections, but of entire unreserve:
it is life's undress rehearsal, its backroom, its dressing room.
-*Harriet Beecher Stowe*

Home is the definition of God.
-*Emily Dickinson*

Home...where we begin, where we grow, where we always
long for, where the love is always a different love
than found anywhere else on earth.
-*Crystal Dawn Perry*

COUSINS

Near or apart, cousins always live in our hearts.

Having a cousin is like having an arranged friendship.
-*Crystal Dawn Perry*

CRAWLING

(see also Firsts)

Oh, the places you'll go!
-Dr. Seuss

By perseverance the snail reached the ark.
-Charles Haddon Spurgeon

Behold the turtle. He makes progress only when he sticks his neck
out.
-James B. Conant

I say, if your knees aren't green by the end of the day,
you ought to seriously re-examine your life.
-Bill Watterson, Calvin & Hobbes

Ambition can creep as well as soar.
-Edmund Burke

CRYING

Tears...the diamonds of the eye.
-Rev. Dr. Davies

It's terribly amusing how many different climates
of feeling one can go through in a day.
-Anne Morrow Lindbergh

Only eyes washed by tears can see clearly.
-Louis L. Mann

The soul would have no rainbow had the eyes no tears.
-John Vance Cheney

The body is a house of many windows: there we all sit, showing
ourselves and crying on the passers-by to come and love us.
-Robert Louis Stevenson

Family...how could a little baby make a family?
How could cooing, crying, stinking, wiping make us more united?
And yet, somehow it does.
-Carl Joseph Vonnoh, OOO

Please forgive me for smiling when I first heard your cry.
It was the most beautiful pitiful sound I had ever heard.
-Crystal Dawn Perry

Where is home? Home is where the heart can laugh without shyness
Home is where the heart's tears can dry at the their own pace.
-Vernon G. Baker

Mad, bad, and dangerous to know.
-Lady Caroline Lamb

What soap is for the body, tears are for the soul.
-Jewish Proverb

DANCE

God dances amidst the common.
-Max Lucado

There was a star that danced, and under that was I born.
-William Shakespeare

If I could tell you what I mean, there would be no point in dancing.
-Isadora Duncan

The infant is music itself.
-Hazrat Inayat Khan

If you can walk, you can dance.
-Zimbabwe saying

DAUGHTER

A daughter can light up your day
simply by blinking her big, bright eyes.
-Crystal Dawn Perry

Little girls are the nicest things that happen to people.
They are born with a little bit of angelshine about them, and though
it wears thin sometimes, there is always enough left to lasso your
heart.
-Allan Beck

A daughter is to her father a treasure of sleeplessness.
-Ben Siva

"Flowers o' the home," says he, "Are daughters."
-Marceline Desbordes-Valmore

A toddling little girl is the center of a common feeling
which makes the most dissimilar people understand each other.
-George Eliot

Who can describe the transports of a heart truly parental on
beholding a daughter shoot up like some fair and modest flower,
and acquire, day after day, fresh beauty and growing sweetness,
so as to fill every eye with pleasure and every heart with admiration.
-James Fordyce

Being a daughter is only half of the equation; bearing one is the other.
-Erica Jong

DAY CARE/PRE-SCHOOL

If there were no schools to take the children away from home part
of the time, the insane asylum would be filled with mothers.
-Edgar Watson Howe

Our human problem – once common to parents, sons and daughters –
is letting go while holding tight
to the unraveling yarn that ties our hearts.
-*Louise Erdrich*

Teaching kids to count is fine, but teaching them what counts is best.
-*Bob Talbert*

To the uneducated, an A is just three sticks.
-*A.A. Milne*

Leaving a child for the first time feels as though we are leaving a
small piece of our heart – the place in our heart where we stored all
of our together times. Immediately, we feel the need to restore it;
desperately hoping that piece of our heart cannot be erased.
-*Crystal Dawn Perry*

D I A P E R S

It is not a fragrant world.
-*Raymond Chandler*

Life is like a diaper. You get out whatever you put in.
And sometimes it stinks.
-*Crystal Dawn Perry*

Diaper backwards spells repaid. Think about it.
-*Marshall McLuhan*

Spread the diaper in the position of the diamond with you at bat.
Then fold second base down to home and set the baby on
the pitcher's mound. Put first base and third together,
bring up home plate and pin the three together. Of course,
in case of rain, you gotta call the game and start all over again.
-*Jimmy Piersal*

Family...how could a little baby make a family?
How could cooing, crying, stinking, wiping make us more united?
And yet, somehow it does.
-*Carl Joseph Vonnoh, ooo*

I have a simple philosophy. Fill what's empty.
Empty what's full. And scratch where it itches.
-Alice Roosevelt Longworth

DIMPLES

I feel about mothers the way I feel about dimples;
because I do not have one myself, I notice everyone who does.
-Letty Cottin Pogrebin

Enchanting is that baby-laugh, all dimples and glitter...
so strangely warm and innocent.
-Margaret F. Ossoli

The little child, when it sees a star sparkle,
stretches out its dimpled arms; it wants that star.
To want a star is the beautiful insanity of the young.
-Countess de Gasparin

DIRTY / MESSY

(see Trouble)

DOG / PUPPY

My little dog – a heartbeat at my feet.
-Edith Wharton

There is no psychiatrist in the world like a puppy licking your face.
-Ben Williams

Dogs laugh, but they laugh with their tails.
-Max Eastman

Dachshunds are the ideal dogs for small children, as they are already
stretched and pulled to such a length that the child cannot do much
harm one way or the other.
-Robert Benchley

DOLLS

The little girl expects no declaration of tenderness from her doll.
She loves it, and that's all. It is thus that we should love.
-De Gourmont

A doll is a best friend that gets sat on, thrown on the floor, dragged
by her hair and carried out in the public with no clothes on, all while
seeming as though there is no place else she would rather be...
It's no wonder she is loved so dearly.
-Crystal Dawn Perry

DRESS - UP

You can grow up to be anything you want to be.

The difference between ordinary and extraordinary is
that little extra.
John Ruskin

Just around the corner in every woman's mind –
is a lovely dress, a wonderful suit, or entire costume which will
make an enchanting new creature of her.
-Wilhela Cushman

Fashion can be bought. Style one must possess.
-Edna Woolman Chase

Style is a simple way of saying complicated things.
Jean Cocteau

Remember that always dressing in understated good taste
is the same as playing dead.
-Susan Catherine

The truly fashionable are beyond fashion.
-Cecil Beaton

It is only when the mind and character slumber
that the dress can be seen.
-*Ralph Waldo Emerson*

E A R S

We have two ears and one mouth so that we
can listen twice as much as we speak.
-*Epictetus*

The eyes believe themselves; the ears believe other people.
-*German proverb*

One of the best ways to persuade others
is with your ears.
-*Dean Rusk*

E A S T E R

Blue skies with white clouds on summer days. A myriad of stars on
clear moonlit nights...bluebirds and laughter and sunshine and
Easter.
See how He loves us!
-*Alice Chaplin*

On Easter Day, the veil between time and eternity thins to gossamer.
-*Douglas Horton*

Put all thine eggs in one basket – and watch that basket.
-*Mark Twain*

The Lord has risen indeed!
St. Luke 24:34 (KJV)

E A T I N G

If only their outfits could be color coordinated with their meals!
-*Connie Berry*

There are times when parenthood seems nothing more
than feeding the mouth that bites you.
-Peter De Vries

Once in a lifetime one should be allowed to have as much sweetness
as one can possibly want and hold.
Judith Obrey

Never eat more than you can lift.
-Miss Piggy

A mother finds out what is meant by "spitting image"
when she tries to feed cereal to her baby.
-Imogene Fay

The times spat at me. I spit back at the times.
-Andrei Voznesensky

There is no love sincerer than the love of food.
-George Bernard Shaw

A smiling face is a half the meal.
-Latvian proverb

...feed me with food convenient for me.
Proverb 30:8 (KJV)

...a man hath no better thing under the sun,
than to eat, and to drink, and to be merry.
Ecclesiastes 8:15 (KJV)

EVERYDAY

Enjoy the little things in life, for one day you may look back
and realize they were the big things.

It is, after all, mostly little, common things that make up our lives.
-Elisabeth Elliot

146

Each day comes bearing its own gifts. Untie the ribbons.
-Ruth Ann Schabacker

Yesterday is history. Tomorrow is a mystery. And today?
Today is a gift. That's why we call it the present.
-Babatunde Olatunji

Love the moment, and the energy of that moment
will spread beyond all boundaries.
-Corita Kent

Surprisingly lively, precious days.
What is there to say except: here they are.
Sifting through my fingers like sand.
Joyce Carol Oates

There is no such thing in anyone's life as an unimportant day.
-Alexander Woollcott

Moments spent listening, talking, playing and sharing together
may be the most important times of all.
-Gloria Gaither

The only way to live is to accept each minute as an unrepeatable
miracle, which is exactly what it is: a miracle and unrepeatable.
-Storm Jameson

Life itself is the most wonderful fairytale.
-Hans Christian Andersen

Nothing is more than this day.
-Goethe

Life begins each morning...each morning is the open door
to a new world – new vistas, new aims, new tryings.
-Leigh Hodges

All the great blessings of my life are present in my thoughts today.
-Phoebe Cary

Every day in a life fills the whole life with expectation and memory.
-C. S. Lewis

These little thoughts are the rustle of leaves;
they leave their whisper of joy in my mind.
-Rabindranath Tagore

Write on your heart that every day is the best day of the year.
-Ralph Waldo Emerson

Life isn't a matter of milestones, but of moments.
-Rose Kennedy

EYES

The eye is the jewel of the body.
-Henry David Thoreau

Seek the wisdom of the ages,
but look at the world through the eyes of a child.
-Ron Wild

There are no seven wonders of the world in the eyes of a child.
There are seven million.
-Walt Streightiff

The sight of you...
is as necessary for me as is the sun for the spring flowers.
-Marguerite of Valois

The eyes believe themselves;
the ears believe other people.
-German proverb

The eyes see only what the mind is prepared to comprehend.
-Robertson Davies

FAMILY / FAMILY TREE / HERITAGE

Family...another word for love.

A happy family is but an earlier heaven.
John Bowring

When you look at your life,
the greatest happinesses are family happinesses.
-Dr. Joyce Brothers

What greater thing is there for human souls than to feel that they
are joined for life – to be with each other in silent unspeakable
memories.
-George Eliot

Family...how could a little baby make a family?
How could cooing, crying, stinking, wiping make us more united?
And yet, somehow it does.
-Carl Joseph Vonnoh, DDD

Families are the most beautiful things in all the world.
-Louisa May Alcott

Other things change us,
but we start and end with the family.
-Anthony Brandt

Family faces are magic mirrors.
Looking at people who belong to us,
we see the past, present and future.
-Gail Lumet Buckley

The family is one of nature's masterpieces.
-George Santayana

A man finds room in a few square inches of his face for the traits of
all his ancestors; for the expression of all his history, and his wants.
-Ralph Waldo Emerson

A man's rootage is more important than his leafage.
-Woodrow Wilson

Deep in their roots, all flowers keep the light.
-Theodore Roethke

The tree of life has many boughs,
where the bird of love may perch and sing!
-Joan Walsh Anglund

I am the vine, ye are the branches.
John 15:5 (KJV)

Lo, children are an heritage of the Lord;
and the fruit of the womb is his reward.
Psalm 127:3 (KJV)

FATHER

I look just like my Daddy.
I have his double chin and a pot belly.

Anyone can be a Father,
but it takes someone special to be a Daddy.

What do I owe my father? Everything.
-Henry Van Dyke

It is much easier to become a father than to be one.
-Kent Nerburn

Of all nature's gifts to the human race,
what is sweeter to a man than his children?
-Marcus Tullius Cicero

He wants to live on through something –
and in his case, his masterpiece is his son.
-Arthur Miller

A daughter is to her father a treasure of sleeplessness.
-Ben Siva

The moon was never so close as when I rode on your shoulders.
-Unknown

The night you were born I ceased being my father's boy
and became my son's father. That night I began a new life.
-Henry Gregor Felson

It is not flesh and blood but the heart which makes us fathers and
sons.
-Schiller

Safe, for a child, is his father's hand, holding him tight.
-Pam Brown

Blessed indeed is the man who hears
many gentle voices call him father!
-Lydia M. Child

Children's children are the crown of old men,
and the glory of children are their father.
Proverbs 17:1 (KJV)

Thou art my Son, this day have I begotten thee?
And again, I will be to him a Father, and he shall be to me a Son.
Hebrews 1:5 (KJV)

FEET

The thumb is, by far, the tastiest of all the fingers.
I'll dare say it even exceeds the taste of toes.
-Crystal Dawn Perry

A tiny foot makes a deep impression.
-Crystal Dawn Perry

FIRSTS

There are no shortcuts to life's greatest achievements.

The difference between try and triumph is a little umph.
-*Unknown*

He who would learn to fly one day must first learn to
stand and walk and run and climb and dance;
one cannot fly into flying.
-*Friedrich Nietzsche*

Nothing in the world can take the place of persistence...
Persistence and determination alone are omnipotent.
-*Calvin Coolidge*

Never, never, never, never give up.
-*Winston Churchill*

Life begins each morning...
each morning is the open door to a new world –
new vistas, new aims, new tryings.
-*Leigh Hodges*

Life isn't a matter of milestones, but of moments.
-*Rose Kennedy*

FOSTER CHILD
(*see also Adoption*)

Most of the important things in the world have been accomplished by
people who have kept on trying when there seemed to be
no hope at all.
-*Dale Carnegie*

A baby is born with a need to be loved - and never outgrows it.
-*Frank A. Clark*

Children have more need of models than of critics.
Joseph Joubert

All children wear the sign: "I want to be important NOW."
Many of our juvenile delinquency problems arise
because nobody reads the sign.
-Dan Pursuit

What loneliness is more lonely than distrust?
-George Eliot

I am I plus my circumstances.
Jose Ortega y Gasset

When one has not had a good father, one must create one.
-Friedrich Nietzsche

For I was hungry and you gave me something to eat,
I was thirsty and you gave me something to drink,
I was a stranger and you invited me in.
Matthew 25:35 (NIV)

GIRLS

(see Daughter)

GODCHILD / GODPARENTS

Few things help an individual more than to place responsibility
upon him, and to let him know that you trust him.
-Booker T. Washington

Few delights can equal the mere presence of one whom
we trust utterly.
-George MacDonald

Responsibility: A detachable burden easily shifted
to the shoulders of God, Fate, Fortune, Luck or one's neighbor.
In the days of astrology, it was customary to unload it upon a star.
-Ambrose Bierce

GRANDCHILDREN /
GRANDPARENTS

Grandchildren are the gifts of yesterday,
the pride of today and the joy of tomorrow.

Grandparents are made in Heaven,
born with the birth of
their first grandchild.

I look just like my Grandpa.
I have his double chin and a pot belly.

A grandmother is a mother who has a second chance.

No cowboy was ever faster on the draw than a
grandparent pulling a baby picture out of a wallet.
-Unknown

Grandchildren are God's way of compensating us for growing old.
-Mary H. Waldrip

Few things are more delightful than
grandchildren fighting over your lap.
-Doug Larson

A baby brings out the love, tolerance and tenderness
which have become rusty with the years.
-F. M. Wightman

A grandmother is a person with way too much wisdom to let that
stop her from making a fool of herself over her grandchildren.
-Phil Moss

I'm a flower...opening and reaching for the sun.
You are the sun, Grandma; you are the sun in my life.
-Kitty Tsui

Mothers of daughters are daughters of mothers and have remained
so, in circles joined to circles, since time began.
-Signe Hammer

A baby has a way of making a man out of his father,
and a boy out of his grandfather.
-Angie Papadakis

The simplest toy, one which even the youngest child can operate,
is called a grandparent.
-Sam Levenson

To the world, they are decades and miles apart but to a
grandparent's soul, the grandchild is only a heartbeat away.
-Crystal Dawn Perry

Grandparents help kids understand and settle into a world
which can be pretty confusing to newcomers.
-Charles Slaybaugh

Children are a great comfort in your old age
– and they help you to reach it faster too.
-Lionel M. Kauffman

We never know the love of our parents for us
'til we have become parents.
-Henry Ward Beecher

One of the most powerful handclasps is that of a new grandbaby
around the finger of a grandfather.
-Joy Hargrove

Grandparents somehow sprinkle a sense
of stardust over grandchildren.
-Alex Haley

Grandparents let you act like a kid.
-Carl Joseph Vonnoh, OOO

If your baby is...
"beautiful and perfect, never cries or fusses, sleeps on schedule and
burps on demand, an angel all the time," you're the grandma.
-Theresa Bloomingdale

A grandfather is a man who can't understand
how his idiot son has such brilliant children.
-Milton Berle

Grandfathers don't count on parents or fairy godmothers
to insure that their grandkids' lives are happy;
they do everything in their power to make them that way.
-Conrad McCoy

Children's children are the crown of old men,
and the glory of children are their father.
Proverbs 17:1 (KJV)

GROWING

It will be gone before you know it.
The fingerprints on the wall appear higher and higher.
Then suddenly they disappear.
-Dorothy Evslin

Who can describe the transports of a heart truly parental on
beholding a daughter shoot up like some fair and
modest flower, and acquire,
day after day, fresh beauty and growing sweetness, so as to fill
every eye with pleasure and every heart with admiration.
-James Fordyce

Good things, when short, are twice a good.
-Baltasar Gracian

The impression you leave on my heart grows as you do.
-Crystal Dawn Perry

Growth is the only evidence of life.
-Cardinal Newman

HAIR / LACK OF / HAIRCUT

Why don't you get a haircut? You look like a chrysanthemum.
-P.G. Wodehouse

Hair is vitally personal to children. They weep vigorously when it is
cut for the first time; no matter how it grows,
bushy, straight or curly,
they feel they are being shorn of a part of their personality.
-Charles Chaplin

No matter how perfect your mother thinks you are,
she will always want to fix your hair.
-Suzanne Beilenson

Bald as the bare mountaintops are bald,
with a baldness full of grandeur.
-Matthew Arnold

There's one thing about baldness – it's neat.
-Don Herold

The most delightful advantage of being bald – one can
hear snowflakes.
-R.G. Daniels

Irrevocable as a haircut.
-Lynwood L. Giacomini

HALF-SIBLING

I don't believe an accident of birth makes people sisters or brothers
It makes them siblings, gives them mutuality of parentage.
Sisterhood and brotherhood is a condition people have to work at.
-Maya Angelou

HALLOWEEN

A grandmother pretends she doesn't know who you are
on Halloween.
-Erma Bombeck

From ghoulies and ghosties and long leggety beasties and
Things that go bump in the night, Good Lord, deliver us!
-Scottish saying

'Tis now the very witching time of night.
-William Shakespeare

HANDS

Who takes the child by the hand, takes the mother by the heart.
-Danish Proverb

When a woman puts her finger for the first time into the tiny hand of
her baby and feels that helpless clutch which tightens her very
heartstrings, she is born again with the newborn child.
-Kate Douglas Wiggin

What feeling is so nice as a child's hand in yours? So small,
so soft and warm, like a kitten huddling in the shelter of your clasp
-Marjorie Holmes

Such tiny hands to hold our hearts forever.
-Pam Brown

HANUKKAH

Hanukkah reminds us that faith can give us
the strength to overcome oppression.
-George Bush

HAPPY BABY
(see also Laughter and Smile)

The time to be happy is now. The place to be happy is here.
-Robert G. Ingersoll

The light of a baby's smile gives a hearty warmth to the soul.
-Crystal Dawn Perry

We find delight in the beauty and happiness of children
that makes the heart too big for the body.
-Ralph Waldo Emerson

Enthusiasm is a divine possession.
-Margaret E. Sangster

A good laugh is sunshine in the house.
-William Makepeace Thackeray

Love is the master key,
which opens the gates of happiness.
-Oliver Wendell Holmes, Sr.

There is only one happiness in life, to love and be loved.
-George Sands

I know well that happiness is in the little things.
-John Ruski

...a man hath no better thing under the sun,
than to eat, and to drink, and to be merry.
Ecclesiastes 8:15 (KJV)

HARDSHIP

There is not enough darkness in the world
to put out the light of even one small candle.
-Robert Alden

I am as my Creator made me, and since He is satisfied, so am I.
-Minnie Smith

I don't think of all the misery but the beauty that still remains.
-Anne Frank

All the world is full of suffering. It is also full of overcoming it.
-Helen Keller

Every problem has a gift for you in its hands.
-Richard Bach

No one tells you that the change is irreversible. That you will feel in
your heart every pain, every loss, every disappointment, every
rebuff, every cruelty that she experiences life long.
-Pam Brown

Where there's life, there's hope.
-Terence

If it were not for hopes, the heart would break.
-Thomas Fuller

Don't cry over things that were or things that aren't.
Enjoy what you have now to the fullest.
-Barbara Bush

Each dawn holds a new hope for a new plan,
making the start of each day the start of a new life.
-Gina Blair

The doctors told me I would never walk, but my mother told me I
would – so I believed my mother.
-Wilma Rudolph

As I watched her at play... it came to me that this
child would pass through life as the angels live in Heaven.
The difficulties of existence would never be hers.
-Pearl S. Buck, of her daughter with special needs

You can complain because roses have thorns,
or you can rejoice because thorns have roses.
-Ziggy

Aerodynamically the bumblebee shouldn't be able to fly,
but the bumblebee doesn't know that so it goes on flying anyway.
-Mary Kay Ash

You have a unique message to deliver, a unique song to sing,
a unique act of love to bestow. This message, this song, and
this act of love have been entrusted exclusively to the one and only
you.
-John Powell

Flowers grow out of dark moments.
-Corita Kent

Faith is the bird that feels the light and
sings when the dawn is still dark.
-Rabindranath Tagore

Hope is the thing with feathers that perches in the soul and
sings the tune without words and never stops at all.
-Emily Dickinson

The angel whose spirit soars so high that it seems unstoppable, is the
hardest on our heart to see lying, wings creased, and spirit broken.
-Crystal Dawn Perry

Never be afraid to trust an unknown future to an all-knowing God.
-Corrie Ten Boom

We shall draw from the heart of suffering itself
the means of inspiration and survival.
-Winston Churchill

Most of the important things in the world have been accomplished by
people who have kept on trying when there seemed to
be no hope at all.
-Dale Carnegie

We do not understand the intricate pattern of the stars in their
courses, but we know that He who created them does, and that just
as surely as He guides them, He is charting a safe course for us.
-Billy Graham

"You almost died," a nurse told her. But that was nonsense.
Of course she wouldn't have died; She had children.
When you have children, you're obligated to live.
-Anne Tyler

The rainbow of God's promises is always above
the trials and storms of life.
-Charles Shepson

As a mother comforts her child, so will I comfort you.
Isaiah 66:13 (NIV)

A cheerful heart is good medicine,
but a crushed spirit dries up the bones.
Proverbs 17:22 (NIV)

HOLDING BABY

There is no experience better for the heart
than reaching down and lifting people up.
-John Andrew Holmer

There is nothing stronger in the world than gentleness.
-Han Suyin

Every baby needs a lap.
-Henry Rabin

Who is getting more pleasure from this rocking, the baby or me?
-Nancy Thayer

We say, "I love you" to our children, but it's not enough.
Maybe that's why mothers hug and hold and rock and kiss and pat.
-Joan McIntosh

I love sitting on your lap. I could sit here all day if
you didn't stand up.
-Groucho Marx

A rich child often sits in a poor mother's lap.
-Spanish proverb

A mother's arms are made of tenderness,
and children sleep soundly in them.
-Victor Hugo

There is no place I'd rather be tonight,
except in my mother's arms.
-Duke Ellington

Once in a lifetime one should be allowed to have as much sweetness
as one can possibly want and hold.
-Judith Obrey

We two form a multitude.
-Ovid

Hold thou me up, and I shall be safe.
Psalm 119:117 (KJV)

HOME BIRTH

(see Coming Home)

HUGS AND KISSES

Kids are like sponges: they absorb all your strength and leave you
limp but give them a squeeze and you get it all back.
-Barbara Johnson

Everyone was meant to share God's all-abiding love and care;
He saw that we would need to know a way to let these feelings show.
so God made hugs.
Jill Wolf

We say, "I love you" to our children, but it's not enough.
Maybe that's why mothers hug and hold and rock and kiss and pat.
Joan McIntosh

There is nothing stronger in the world than gentleness.
-Han Suyin

The only thing worth stealing is a kiss from a sleeping child.
Joe Houldsworth

ILLNESS

(see also Hardship)

Being sick is no fun but I sure like the attention!
-Carl Joseph Vonnoh, III

A smart mother makes often a better diagnosis than a poor doctor.
-August Bier

The angel whose spirit soars so high that it seems unstoppable, is the
hardest on our heart to see lying, wings creased, and spirit broken.
-Crystal Dawn Perry

To be sick is to enjoy monarchal prerogatives.
-Charles Lamb

Most things get better by themselves.
Most things, in fact, are better by morning.
-Lewis Thomas

I was sick and ye visited me.
St. Matthew 25:31 (KJV)

INDEPENDENCE DAY

Patriotism is not short, frenzied outbursts of emotion,
but the tranquil and steady dedication of a lifetime.
-Adlai Stevenson

If our American way of life fails the child, it fails us all.
-Pearl S. Buck

What is patriotism but the love of the food one ate as a child?
-Lin Yutang

INJURY
(see also Hardship)

The angel whose spirit soars so high, it seems unstoppable, is the
hardest on our heart to see lying, wings creased and spirit broken.
-Crystal Dawn Perry

Most things get better by themselves.
Most things, in fact, are better by morning.
-Lewis Thomas

Write injuries in sand, kindnesses in marble.
-French Proverb

The only comfort better than a mother's is a colorful bandage.
-Crystal Dawn Perry

Woe is me for my hurt!
Jeremiah 10:19 (KJV)

LAUGHTER
(see also *Happy Baby* and *Smile*)

"When the first baby laughed for the first time,
the laugh broke into thousands of pieces
and they all went skipping about,
and that was the beginning of fairies."
James M. Barrie

Life's song would be a tuneless dirge
without the sound of children's laughter.
John Beith

When we hear the baby laugh,
it is the loveliest thing that can happen to us.
-Sigmund Freud

A child's laughter reminds us what it was like to be little.
-Carl Joseph Vonnoh, OOO

Enchanting is that baby-laugh, all dimples and glitter...
so strangely warm and innocent.
-Margaret F. Ossoli

Babies have laughs that are totally inappropriate to their size –
huge guffaws, rumbles of delight, squeals of excitement,
rich and rounded gigglings.
-Pam Brown

LOVE

A child's love is like the dawn unfolding... bright,
new and full of hope.

The more love you give to your children,
the more love they will have to give.
-Crystal Dawn Perry

Love is the master key, which opens the gates of happiness.
-Oliver Wendell Holmes, Sr.

Ultimately, love is everything.
-M. Scott Peck

There is only one happiness in life: to love and be loved.
-George Sands

Give a little love to a child, and you get a great deal back.
J. Ruskin

Love is that condition in which the happiness
of another person is essential to your own.
-Robert Heinlein

It is not a slight thing when they, who are so fresh from God, love us.
-Charles Dickens

Love is like a rainbow...an intangible beauty that leaves us
feeling as though we've been hugged by God's grace.
-Crystal Dawn Perry

Where there is great love, there are always miracles.
-Willa Cather

Yours is the light by which my spirit's born.
-E. E. Cummings

When you love someone, all your saved-up wishes start coming out.
-Elizabeth Bowen

Who, being loved, is poor?
-Oscar Wilde

The love of a child is trusting, sincere, and all encompassing.
As a parent, we can only hope that when our child looks into our
eyes, these emotions are reflected and engulfed.
-Crystal Dawn Perry

MEMORIES

The heart hath its own memory, like the mind,
and in it are enshrined the precious keepsakes.

These little thoughts are the rustle of leaves;
they leave their whisper of joy in my mind.
-Rabindranath Tagore

Happy times and bygone days are never lost...
In truth, they grow more wonderful within the heart that keeps
them.
-Kay Andrews

Recall it as often as you wish; a happy memory never wears out.
-Libbie Fudim

Each happiness of yesterday is a memory for tomorrow.
-George Webster Douglas

What we have once enjoyed we can never lose.
All that we love deeply becomes a part of us.
-Helen Keller

God has given us our memories that we might have roses in
December.
-J.M. Barrie

MEMORY OF A LOVED ONE
(see also Memories)

Early, bright, transient, chaste as morning dew,
She sparkled, was exhal'd and went to heaven.
-Edward Young

She weeps for him a mother's burning tears –
she loved him with a mother's deepest love.
-Paul Laurence Dunbar

Look for me in the nurseries of Heaven.
-*Francis Thompson*

To live in hearts we leave behind is not to die.
-*Thomas Campbell*

MOTHER

A mother's children are portraits of herself.

Motherhood is an experience that opens your eyes and your heart
to exactly how magnificent and amazing the gift of life is.
-*Donna Newman*

A mother is not a person; she's a miracle.
-*Mary Hollingsworth*

The purpose of life is a life of purpose.
-*Robert Byrne*

A mother's love for her child is like nothing else in the world.
It knows no law, no pity; it dares all things and crushes down
remorselessly all that stands in its path.
-*Agatha Christie*

A mother's heart is a baby's most beautiful dwelling.
-*Ed Dussault*

Who is it that loves me and will love me forever with an affection
which no chance, no misery, no crime of mine can do away?
It is you, my mother.
-*Thomas Carlyle*

Motherhood: All love begins and ends there.
-*Robert Browning*

There's no way to be a perfect mother
and a million ways to be a good one.
-*Jill Churchill*

Is not a young mother one of the sweetest sights life shows us?
-William Makepeace Thackeray

Where there is great love, there is always a mother nearby.
-Norma Scarlett

Women know the way to rear up children ...
They know a simple, merry, tender knack of tying sashes,
fitting baby shoes, and stringing pretty words that make no sense,
and kissing full sense into empty words.
-Elizabeth Barrett Browning

She is their earth, she is their food and their bed
and the extra blanket when it grows cold in the night;
she is their warmth and their health and their shelter.
-Katherine Butler Hathaway

Children are what the mothers are. No fondest father's fondest care
can fashion so the infant heart.
-Walter Savage Landor

I think my life began with waking up and loving mother's face.
-George Eliot

The goodness of a home is not dependent on wealth, or spaciousness
or beauty, or luxury. Everything depends on the Mother.
-G.W. Russell

A woman who can cope with the terrible twos can cope with
anything.
Judith Clabes

Judicious mothers will always keep in mind that they are
the first book read, and the last put aside in every child's library.
-C. Lenox Remond

A mother's arms are made of tenderness,
and children sleep soundly in them.
-Victor Hugo

Mother is the name for God in the lips and hearts of children.
-William Makepeace Thackeray

Nothing else will ever make you as happy or as sad,
as proud or as tired, as motherhood.
-Elia Parsons

There is no other closeness in human life like
the closeness between a mother and her baby:
chronologically, physically, and spiritually,
they are just a few heartbeats away
from being the same person.
-Susan Cheever

A mother understands what a child does not say.
-Jewish proverb

Her children arise up, and call her blessed.
Proverbs 31:28

MOUTH

A baby's lips...the shape of angel wings.
-Crystal Dawn Perry

MULTIPLES
(see also Siblings)

We two form a multitude.
-Ovid

A multiple birth is like putting one quarter into
the bouncy ball machine and getting more than just one toy.
You may not get the colors you wanted but
you're still pretty thrilled by your luck!
-Carl Joseph Vonnoh, III

Raising children is like making biscuits:
it is as easy to raise a big batch as one,
while you have your hands in the dough.
-E.W. Howe

The creation of a thousand forests is in one acorn.
-Ralph Waldo Emerson

Every crowd has a silver lining.
-P.T. Barnum

It is because we are different that each of us is special.
-Brian Dyson

There are two things in life for which we are never
fully prepared, and that is twins.
-Josh Billings

Double, double toil and trouble.
-William Shakespeare

All who would win joy must share it;
happiness was born a twin.
Lord Byron (1711 - 1824)

Laughter and crying are twin experiences.
-Ai Bei

NAME

What's in a name?
That which we call a rose by any other name would smell as sweet.
-William Shakespeare

No matter what a child is named, at some point in life,
the child will hate it...not a particularly comforting thought to
the parents that tormented over it for nine months.
-Crystal Dawn Perry

Any child can tell you that the sole purpose of a middle name
is so he can tell when he's really in trouble.
-Dennis Fakes

Life is for one generation; a good name is forever.
-Jewish Proverb

This is my name forever, the name by which I am to be remembered
from generation to generation.
Exodus 3:15 (NIV)

NEW YEAR

We meet today to thank Thee for the era done,
and Thee for the opening one.
-John Greenleaf Whittier

The merry year is born, like the bright berry from the naked thorn.
-Hartley Coleridge

NOSE

He that has a great nose thinks everybody is speaking of it.
-Thomas Fuller

That's the most precious button I've ever seen
...and it goes with everything!
-Crystal Dawn Perry

NUDITY

There is a crack in everything that God has made.
-Ralph Waldo Emerson

Of all the things you wear, your expression is the most important.
-Janet Lane

Nudity, among babies, is still socially acceptable.
-Carl Joseph Vonnoh, OOO

Clothes make the man.
Naked people have little or no influence on society.
-Mark Twain

Every man has his moral backside too,
which he doesn't expose unnecessarily but keeps covered
as long as possible by the trousers of decorum.
-G.C. Lichtenberg

Most things in life are moments of pleasure
and a lifetime of embarrassment;
photography is a moment of embarrassment
and a lifetime of pleasure.
-Tony Benn

The finest clothing made is a person's skin, but, of course,
society demands something more than this.
-Mark Twain

NURSERY

Rocking chair, crib and blanket...
all waiting to comfort a dream.
-Crystal Dawn Perry

The nursery is the foundation of all beginnings.
-Crystal Dawn Perry

ONLY CHILD

Solitary trees, if they grow at all, grow strong.
-Winston Churchill

I was never less alone than when by myself.
-Edward Gibbon

PACIFIER/THUMB

The chains of habit are generally too small to be felt
until they are too strong to be broken.
-Samuel Johnson

Habit is stonger than reason.
-George Santayana

The thumb is, by far, the tastiest of all the fingers.
I'll dare say it even exceeds the taste of toes.
-Crystal Dawn Perry

Vice goes a long way toward making life bearable.
A little vice now and then is relished by the best of men.
-Finley Peter Dunne

PARENTHOOD

erhaps the greatest social service that can be rendered by anybody
to the country and to mankind is to bring up a family.
-George Bernard Shaw

We never know the love of our parents for us until we become
parents. When we first bend over the cradle of our own child, God
throws back the temple door, and reveals to us the sacredness and
mystery
of a father's and a mother's love to ourselves.
-Henry Ward Beecher

It takes love and grit to raise a child and the heart of a tempered
soul.
-Connie Berry

Having a baby is like falling in love again,
both with your husband and your child.
-Tina Brown

There are times when parenthood seems nothing more
than feeding the hand that bites you.
-Peter De Vries

Parenthood remains the greatest single preserve of the amateur.
-Alvin Toffler

While we try to teach our children all about life,
our children teach us what life is all about.
-Angel Schwindt

The love of a child is trusting, sincere, and all encompassing.
As a parent, we can only hope that when our child looks into our
eyes, these emotions are reflected and engulfed.
-Crystal Dawn Perry

The best combination of parents consists of a father who is gentle
beneath his firmness, and a mother who is firm beneath her
gentleness.
-Sydney Harris

Parents are the bones on which children cut their teeth.
-Peter Ustinov

Train up a child in the way he should go,
and when he is old, he will not depart from it.
Proverbs 22:1 (KJV)

PASSOVER

Let all who are hungry come in and eat,
let all who are needy come and make Passover.
-Haggadah

This historic event became a theological paradigm that pointed to
future redemption and took on cosmic proportions.
-Philip Sigal

And thus shall ye eat it; with your loins girded, your shoes on your
feet, and your staff in your hand; and ye shall eat it in haste:
it is the Lord's Passover.
Exodus 12:11

PET

Our perfect companions never have fewer than four feet.
-Colette

A pet is baby's first best friend.
-Crystal Dawn Perry

Animals are such agreeable friends –
they ask no questions, they pass no criticisms.
-George Eliot

PLAY / PLAY GROUP
(see also Toys)

The language of friendship is not words but meanings.
-Henry David Thoreau

We have been friends together in sunshine and in shade.
-Caroline Sheridan Norton

Since there is nothing so well worth having as friends,
never lose a chance to make them.
-Francesco Guicciardini

I have friends in overalls whose friendship I would not swap
for the favor of the kings of the world.
-Thomas A. Edison

PLAYPEN

A playpen holds a child captive so that the parent is set free.
-Crystal Dawn Perry

The more you let yourself go, the less others let you go.
-Friedrich Nietzche

POSING FOR CAMERA

A good snapshot stops a moment from running away.
-Eudora Welty

Posing for the camera only proves to others how beautiful I am.
I already know it.
-Carl Joseph Vonnoh, OOO

Self-confidence is the first requisite to great undertakings.
-Samuel Johnson

Most things in life are moments of pleasure
and a lifetime of embarrassment;
photography is a moment of embarrassment and a
lifetime of pleasure.
-Tony Benn

Photographers deal in things which are continually vanishing,
and when they have vanished, there is no contrivance on earth
which can make them come back again.
-Henri Cartier Bresson

PREGNANCY

Is not a young mother one of the sweetest sights life shows us?
-William Makepeace Thackeray

Change always comes bearing gifts.
-Price Pritchett

The slow rhythm of waiting.
-Adrian Cowell

Being a daughter is only half of the equation; bearing
one is the other.
-Erica Jong

To me, the only answer a woman can make to the destructive forces of the world is creation. And the most ecstatic form of creation is the creation of new life.

Jessie Bernard

Little fish, you kick and dart and glide beneath my ribs as if they were your private reef.

-Ethna McKiernan

The only time a woman wishes she were a year older is when she is carrying a baby.

-Mary Marsh

To me, life is tough enough without having someone kick you from the inside.

-Rita Rudner

If pregnancy were a book, they would cut the last two chapters.

-Nora Ephron

I never feel so good as when I'm pregnant. It's the only time a woman can sit still, do nothing at all, and still be beautifully productive.

-Maria Riva

It is a long road from conception to completion.

-Moliere

By far the most common craving of pregnant women is not to be pregnant.

-Phyllis Diller

Every crowd has a silver lining.

-P.T. Barnum

Pregnancy makes me wonder why I dieted for two months before the wedding.

Carl Joseph Vonnoh, III

PREMATURE BIRTH

(see also Hardship)

God screens us evermore from premature ideas.
Our eyes are holden that we cannot see things that stare us in the
face, until the hour arrives that the mind is ripened; then we behold
them and the time when we saw them not is like a dream.
-*Ralph Waldo Emerson*

They tell me that you were born premature, my child, but this is only
partially true...for in my heart, you were right on time.
-*Carl Joseph Vonnoh, OOO*

A person's a person, no matter how small.
-*Dr. Seuss*

The early dew woos the half-opened flowers.
-*Unknown*

Coming early is not just as good as coming at the right moment.
-*Chinese Proverb*

RAISING HEAD

To get the best perspective on life,
one should view it from different angles.
-*Crystal Dawn Perry*

Behold the turtle. He makes progress only when he sticks
his neck out.
-*James B. Conant*

ROLLING OVER

To get the best perspective on life,
one should view it from different angles.
-*Crystal Dawn Perry*

A rolling stone gathers no moss.
-*Publilius Syrus*

Heaven is under our feet, as well as over our heads.
-Henry David Thoreau

People are not disturbed by things, but by the view they take of
them.
-Epictetus

RUNNING
(see Walking)

SANTA CLAUS
(see also Christmas)

More than Santa Claus,
your sister knows when you've been bad or good.
-Linda Sunshine

SCRAPBOOKING

There is a time to be born and a time to die,
A time to laugh and a time to cry,
But there never seems to be enough time to scrapbook!

The heart hath its own memory, like the mind,
and in it are enshrined the precious keepsakes.

How will our children know who they are
if they don't know where they came from?
-Ma, Grapes of Wrath

Recall it as often as you wish, a happy memory never wears out.
-Libbie Fudim

Each happiness of yesterday is a memory for tomorrow.
-George Webster Douglas

SIBLING

(see also Brother, Multiples and Sister)

Are we not like two volumes of one book?
-*Marceline Desbordes-Valmore*

Siblings are the people we practice on, the people who teach us
about fairness and cooperation and kindness and caring
- quite often the hard way.
-*Pamela Dugdale*

Blessed indeed is the man who hears
many gentle voices call him father!
-*Lydia M. Child*

SINGLE - PARENTING

When you have a good mother and no father, God kind of sits in.
It's not enough, but it helps.
-*Dick Gregory*

Babies don't need fathers, but mothers do.
Someone who is taking care of a baby needs to be taken care of.
-*Amy Heckerling*

If you can't hold children in your arms, please hold
them in your hearts.
-*Mother Clara Hale*

SIPPY CUP

(see Bottle)

SISTER

A Sister is a special gift of Love.

Is solace anywhere more comforting than in the arms of a sister?
-*Alice Walker*

Bless you, my darling, and remember you are always in the heart
- oh, tucked so close there is no chance of escape - of your sister.
-Katherine Mansfield

Sisters share the scent and smells - the feel of a common childhood.
-Pam Brown

Of two sisters one is always the watcher, one the dancer.
-Louise Gluck

Between sisters, often, the child's cry never dies down.
"Never leave me," it says; "do not abandon me."
-Louise Bernikow

A sister is a gift to the heart, a friend to the spirit,
a golden thread to the meaning of life.
-Isadora James

More than Santa Claus,
your sister knows when you've been bad or good.
-Linda Sunshine

SLEEP

I have spread my dreams under your feet;
Tread softly because you tread on my dreams.
-W.B. Yeats

Sleep, riches and health, to be truly enjoyed must be interrupted.
-Jean Paul Richter

Baby's fishing for a dream, Fishing near and far,
His line a silver moonbeam, His bait a silver star.
-Alice C.D. Riley

The feeling of sleepiness when you are not in bed,
and can't get there, is the meanest feeling in the world.
-Edgar Watson Howe

In the evening, after she has gone to sleep,
I kneel beside the crib and touch her face,
where it is pressed against the slats, with mine.
Joan Didion

The Joy of Motherhood:
What a mom experiences when all the kids are finally in bed.
-Barbara Johnson

A mother's arms are made of tenderness,
and children sleep soundly in them.
-Victor Hugo

There never was a child so lovely
but his mother was glad to get him asleep.
-Ralph Waldo Emerson

People who say they sleep like babies usually don't have them.
-Leo J. Burke

There is not innocent sleep so innocent as sleep shared between a
woman and a child, the little breath hurrying beside the longer.
-Alice Meynel

A daughter is to her father a treasure of sleeplessness.
-Ben Siva

No day is so bad it can't be fixed with a nap.
-Carrie Snow

The only thing worth stealing is a kiss from a sleeping child.
Joe Houldsworth

When I lie down I think, "How long before I get up?"
The night drags on, and I toss till dawn.
Job 7:4 (NIV)

Yet a little sleep, a little slumber, a little folding of the hands to sleep.
Proverbs 1:10 (KJV)

S M I L E

(see also Happy Baby and Laughter)

A smile is a whisper of a laugh.
-A child's definition

There is nothing like a child's smile to make all the chaos
worthwhile.
-Connie Berry

A smile takes but a moment, but its effects sometimes last forever.
J. E. Smith

No one on earth really deserves a baby's radiant smile of recognition.
-Charlotte Gray

The joy of the heart makes the face merry.
-English Proverb

It's terribly amusing how many different climates of feeling
one can go through in a day.
-Anne Morrow Lindbergh

S O N

One good reason why a little boy gets so dirty: he's closer to the
ground.
-Unknown

Love and wonder and rugged splendor...
that's what little boys are really made of.
-Crystal Dawn Perry

Boys are found everywhere – on top of, underneath, inside of,
climbing on, swinging from, running around or jumping to.
-Alan Beck

He wants to live on through something,
and in his case, his masterpiece is his son.
-Arthur Miller

Your little boy is your captor, your jailer, your boss and your
master – a freckle-faced, pint-sized, cat-chasing bundle of noise.
-Alan Beck

It is not flesh and blood, but the heart, which makes
us fathers and sons.
-Schiller

Sons are the anchors of a mother's life.
-Sophocles

The night you were born, I ceased being
my father's boy and became my son's father.
That night I began a new life.
-Henry Gregor Felson

Mothers tend to encourage their sons to run away and romp.
Mothers of little boys often complain, "There's no controlling him.
He's all over the place." It's almost as though the mother enjoyed
being overwhelmed by her spectacular conquering hero.
-Louise J. Kaplan

Thou art my Son, this day have I begotten thee?
And again, I will be to him a Father, and he shall be to me a Son.
Hebrews 1:5 (KJV)

SPECIAL NEEDS
(see Hardship)

ST. PATRICK'S DAY

May good luck be with you wherever you go,
and your blessings outnumber the shamrocks that grow.
-Irish proverb

STANDING / PULLING UP

If you don't stand for something,
you'll fall for anything.

You can either stand up and be counted
or lie down and be counted out.

Our greatest glory is not in never failing,
but in rising up every time we fail.
-Ralph Waldo Emerson

The greatest oak was once a little nut who held its ground.
-Author Unknown

Fall seven times, stand up eight.
Japanese proverb

Where we stand is not as important
as the direction in which we are going.
-Oliver Wendell Holmes, Jr.

A home with a child that can pull up on furniture
always has clean end tables. If the parents don't clean them
off first, the child surely will.
-Crystal Dawn Perry

When sisters stand shoulder to shoulder,
who stands a chance against us?
-Pam Brown

Building blocks, like learning to stand...
the higher you get, the harder the fall.
-Crystal Dawn Perry

My downfall raises me to infinite heights.
-Napoleon Bonaparte

STAY - AT - HOME MOM

Don't make a living at the expense of life.

There is no such thing as a nonworking mother.
-Hester Mundis

Stay, stay at home, my heart, and rest;
Homekeeping hearts are happiest.
-Longfellow

By large, mothers and housewives are the only workers who do not
have regular time off. They are the great vacation-less class.
-Anne Morrow Lindbergh

The work will wait while you show the child the rainbow;
but the rainbow won't wait while you do the work.
-Patricia Clafford

The toughest thing about being a housewife is
you have no place to stay home from.
-Patricia C. Beudoin

Most baby books tend to romanticize the mother who stays
at home as if she really spends her entire day doing
nothing but beaming at the baby and whipping up
educational toys from pieces of string, rather than
balancing cooing time with laundry, cleaning,
shopping and cooking.
-Susan Chira

Being a full-time mother is one of the highest salaried jobs in my
field, since the payment is pure love.
-Mildred B. Vermont

STEP-PARENT / STEP-SIBLING

I don't believe an accident of birth makes people sisters or brothers. It makes them siblings, gives them mutuality of parentage. Sisterhood and brotherhood is a condition people have to work at.
-Maya Angelou

When one has not had a good father, one must create one.
-Friedrich Nietzsche

TALKING

It is often the most intelligible words of babies that speak the most clearly to our heart.
-Crystal Dawn Perry

To the good listener, half a word is enough.
-Spanish proverb

Look wise, say nothing, and grunt. Speech was given to conceal thought.
-William Osler

Pretty much all the honest truth telling there is in the world is done by children.
-Oliver Wendell Holmes

Grant me the power of saying things too simple and too sweet for words.
-Coventry Patmore

He has the gift of quiet.
-John Le Carre

Words should be weighed and not counted.
-Yiddish Proverb

Well done is better than well said.
-Benjamin Franklin

We spend the first twelve months of our children's lives teaching
them to walk and talk and the next twelve telling them to sit down
and shut up. First you have to teach a child to talk,
then you have to teach it to be quiet.
-Prochnow

No one appreciates the very special genius
of your conversation as a dog does.
-Christopher Morley

A mother understands what a child does not say.
Jewish proverb

The walks and talks we have with our two-year-olds in red boots
have a great deal to do with the values they will cherish as adults.
-Edith F. Hunter

Half the world is composed of people who have something to say and
can't, and the other half who have nothing to say and keep on saying
it.
-Robert Frost

Ma-ma does everything for the baby,
who responds by saying Da-da first.
-Mignon McLaughlin

Pleasant words are as an honeycomb,
sweet to the soul, and health to the bones.
Proverb 16:24 (KJV)

TEDDY BEAR

I bear a little more than I can bear.
-Elinor Hoyt Wylie

Loneliness can be conquered only by those who can bear solitude.
-Paul Tillich

Animals are such agreeable friends –
they ask no questions, they pass no criticisms.
-George Eliot

Lots of people talk to animals.... Not very many listen, though....
That's the problem.
-*Benjamin Hoff*

TEETH / TEETHING

Adam and Eve had many advantages,
but the principal one was that they escaped teething.
-*Mark Twain*

The tongue ever turns to the aching tooth.
-*Proverb*

For there was never yet a philosopher that could
endure the toothache patiently.
-*William Shakespeare*

If you can't bite, don't show your teeth.
-*Old Saying*

Parents are the bones on which children cut their teeth.
-*Peter Ustinov*

...there shall be weeping and gnashing of teeth.
Matthew 8:12 (KJV)

THANKSGIVING

There is something in every season,
in every day, to celebrate with thanksgiving.
-*Gloria Gaither*

There's always something for which to be thankful.
-*Charles Dickens*

Thanksgiving is a day for giving thanks and eating pie.
But mainly for eating pie.
-*Carl Joseph Vonnoh, III*

From the fullness of his grace we have all received
one blessing after another.
-John 1:16 (NIV)

In every thing give thanks.
-Thessalonians 5:18 (KJV)

TODDLER

(see also Child/Children)

A toddler is all no-ing.
-Crystal Dawn Perry

A child is a curly, dimpled lunatic.
-Ralph Waldo Emerson

Bright, beautiful, full of pleasure.
Once they are ready to take off, there is no holding them back...
A toddler is fireworks with hair.
-Crystal Dawn Perry

A toddling little girl is the center of a common feeling
which makes the most dissimilar people understand each other.
-George Eliot

The fundamental job of a toddler is to rule the universe.
-Lawrence Kutner

I embrace emerging experience. I participate in discovery.
I am a butterfly. I am not a butterfly collector.
I want the experience of a butterfly.
-William Stafford

This free-will business is a bit terrifying anyway.
It's almost pleasanter to obey, and make the most of it.
-Ugo Betti

I am better than my reputation.
-Friedrich von Schiller

A woman who can cope with the terrible twos can cope with
anything.
Judith Clabes

If you ask me what I came into this world to do,
I will tell you: I came to live out loud.
-Emile Zola

Give curiosity freedom.
-Eudora Welty

Life is the first gift, love is the second, and understanding the third.
-Marge Piercy

We spend the first twelve months of our children's lives teaching
them to walk and talk and the next twelve telling them to sit down
and shut up. First you have to teach a child to talk,
then you have to teach it to be quiet.
-Prochnow

The walks and talks we have with our two-year-olds in red boots
have a great deal to do with the values they will cherish as adults.
-Edith F. Hunter

The simple beauty of a toddler
is greater than every artistic masterpiece combined.
-Carl Joseph Vonnoh, OOO

TOILET TRAINING

We must die to one life before we can enter into another.
-Anatole France

When I'm in the bathroom looking at my toilet paper,
I'm like "Wow! That's toilet paper?"
I don't know if we appreciate how much we have.
-Alicia Silverstone

Train up a child in the way he should go;
and when he is old, he will not depart from it.
Proverb 22:1 (KJV)

TOYS

You will always be your child's favorite toy.
-Vicki Lansky

What we play is life.
-Louis Armstrong

Moments spent listening, talking, playing, and sharing together
may be the most important times of all.
-Gloria Gaither

To live life to its fullest extent,
you must allow your inner child to play to her heart's content.
-Crystal Dawn Perry

An unbreakable toy is good for breaking other toys.
-John Peers

It is in games that many men discover their paradise.
-Robert Lynd

TRADITION

Tradition gives us a sense of solidarity and roots,
a knowing there are some things one can count on.
-Gloria Gaither

Tradition is a form of promise from parent to child.
It's a way to say, "I love you," "I'm here for you," and
"Some things will not change."
-Lynn Ludwick

What an enormous magnifier is tradition!
How a thing grows in the human memory and in the human
imagination, when love, worship, and all that lies in
the human heart, is there to encourage it.
-Thomas Carlyle

TRAVEL

In America there are two classes of travel: first class and with
children.
-Robert Benchley

All traveling becomes dull in exact proportion to its rapidity.
-John Rusk

And that's the wonderful thing about family travel:
it provides you with experiences that will remain locked forever
in the scar tissue of your mind.
-Dave Barry

A good traveler has no fixed plans, and is not intent on arriving.
-Lao Tzu

The traveler was active; he went strenuously in search of people,
of adventure, of experience.
-Daniel J. Boorstin

Though we travel the world over to find the beautiful,
we must carry it with us or we find it not.
-Ralph Waldo Emerson

To travel hopefully is better than to arrive.
-Sir James Jeans

Oh, the places you'll go!
-Dr. Seuss

She never quite leaves her children at home,
even when she doesn't take them along.
-Margaret Culkin Banning

TROUBLE

One good reason why a little boy gets so dirty: he's closer to the ground.

If you obey all the rules, you miss all the fun.
-Katherine Hepburn

I am as bad as the worst, but, Thank God, I am as good as the best.
-Walt Whitman

Dirt is matter out of place.
Oliver Lodge

I learned long ago never to wrestle with a pig.
You get dirty, and besides, the pig likes it.
-Cyrus Ching

Mother had a thousand thoughts to get through within a day, and most of these were about avoiding disaster.
-Natalie Kusz

A toast to Mother – may she live long enough to forget what little fiends we used to be.
-Herbert Prochnow

I believe in getting into hot water; it keeps you clean.
-G.K. Chesterton

A sense of wrongdoing is an enhancement of pleasure.
-Oliver Wendell Holmes, Jr.

A baby up to no good can, without a word, exclaim
"Me? But I'm only a baby!"
-Pam Brown

Things forbidden have a secret charm.
-Tacitus

I have a simple principle for the conduct of life –
never resist an adequate temptation.
-Max Lerner

A baby is always more trouble than you thought – and more
wonderful.
-Charles Osgood

Forgiveness is the answer to the child's dream of a miracle
by which what is broken is made whole again.
-Dag Hammarskjold

ULTRASOUND
(see also Baby)

It is strangely miraculous to see and to hold a living
being formed within oneself and issued forth from oneself.
-Simone de Beauvoir

Life itself is the most wonderful fairytale.
-Hans Christian Andersen

A mother's heart is a baby's most beautiful dwelling.
-Ed Dussault

Little fish, you kick and dart and glide beneath my ribs
as if they were your private reef.
-Ethna McKiernan

In all things of nature there is something of the marvelous.
-Aristotle

A person's a person, no matter how small.
-Dr. Seuss

It is a long road from conception to completion.
-Moliere

The eyes see only what the mind is prepared to comprehend.
-Robertson Davies

With time and patience, the mulberry leaf becomes a silk gown.
-*Chinese proverb*

Change always comes bearing gifts.
-*Price Pritchett*

To me, the only answer a woman can make to the
destructive forces of the world is creation. And the
most ecstatic form of creation
is the creation of new life.
Jessie Bernard

My frame was not hidden from you
when I was made in the secret place.
Psalm 139:15 (NIV)

Lo, children are an heritage of the Lord:
and the fruit of the womb is his reward.
Psalms 127:3 (KJV)

VACATION

Children are the keys of paradise.
-*Richard Stoddard*

It isn't how much time you spend somewhere
that makes it memorable; it's how you spend the time.
-*David Bremer*

VALENTINE'S DAY
(see also Love)

There is nothing so sweet -not flowers, not chocolate,
not a thoughtful card- as the love of a small child that
can be held in the heart on Valentine's Day
and on every day thereafter.
-*Crystal Dawn Perry*

WALKING

Every little step gets us closer to where we're going.

Fall seven times, stand up eight.
Japanese proverb

How can this tiny step,
laid on the floor with all the weight of a swift breeze,
leave such a deep impression on one's heart?
-Crystal Dawn Perry

We spend the first twelve months of our children's lives
teaching them to walk and talk and the next twelve
telling them to sit down and shut up. First you have
to teach a child to talk,then you have
to teach it to be quiet.
-Prochnow

Our greatest glory is not in never failing,
but in rising up every time we fail.
-Ralph Waldo Emerson

Be not afraid of going slowly; be afraid only of standing still.
-Chinese Proverb

One can never consent to creep when one feels an impulse to soar.
-Helen Keller

Remember, we all stumble, every one of us.
That's why it's a comfort to go hand in hand.
-Emily Kimbrough

A journey of a thousand miles must begin with a single step.
-Chinese proverb

By perseverance the snail reached the ark.
-Charles Haddon Spurgeon

The distance is nothing. It's only the first step that's important.
-Marquise Du Deffand

The walks and talks we have with our two-year-olds in red boots
have a great deal to do with the values they will cherish as adults.
-Edith F. Hunter

Go confidently in the direction of your dreams.
-Henry David Thoreau

If you can walk, you can dance.
-Zimbabwe saying

Don't be afraid to take big steps.
-David Lloyd George

That's one small step for man, one giant leap for mankind.
-Neil Armstrong

WORKING MOTHER

Be glad of life because it gives you the chance to love, and to work,
and to play and to look up at the stars.
-Henry Can Dyke

Mother, Food, Love, and Career...the four major guilt groups.
-Cathy Guiswite

The work will wait while you show the child the rainbow;
but the rainbow won't wait while you do the work.
-Patricia Clafford

The phrase "working mother" is redundant.
-Jane Sellman

She never quite leaves her children at home,
even when she doesn't take them along.
-Margaret Culkin Banning

At work, you think of the children you have left at home.
At home, you think of the work left unfinished.
Such a struggle is unleashed within yourself. Your heart is rent.
-Golda Meir

Nobody objects to a woman being a good writer or sculptor or
geneticist if at the same time she manages to be a good wife, good
mother,
good looking, good tempered, well groomed and unaggressive.
-Leslie M. McIntyre

Being asked to decide between your passion for work and your
passion for children is like being asked by your doctor whether you
prefer him to remove your brain or your heart.
-Mary Kay Blakely

Women do no have to sacrifice personhood if they are mothers.
They do not have to sacrifice motherhood in order to be persons.
-Elaine Heffer

We mothered this nation...
and we have no intention of abandoning our roles as nurturer or
wife, mother, loving daughter, tax-paying citizen, homemaker,
breadwinner.
-Liz Carpenter

Quotes

Quotes

Quotes